BUILDING A LIFE AROUND FOOD & COMMUNITY

THE
EDIBLE
GARDEN

COOKBOOK &
GROWING
GUIDE

PAUL WEST

**HOST OF
RIVER COTTAGE
AUSTRALIA**

plum. Pan Macmillan Australia

CONTENTS

INTRODUCTION

I didn't grow up in what you'd call a 'foodie' household. Mum and Dad ran a small business and, on top of that, Dad also worked in the coal mines of the Hunter Valley. They were very busy people and didn't have the luxury of being able to spend a lot of time in the kitchen. That's not to say we didn't eat great food; it's more that food had a utilitarian purpose rather than a gourmet one.

Our town was quite small with few options for takeaway, so every night without fail, Mum would close the shop at 5 pm, come home and have a home-cooked meal on the table by 6 pm. Mum and Dad never discussed business at the table, there were no smart phones and the TV was always off. I look back now and realise how important these meals were to our family. It was a chance to put the day behind us, share our stories and eat nourishing food in good company.

While I've always enjoyed eating good food, it wasn't until I was in my early twenties that I finally discovered the joy of growing food. I was travelling around Tasmania and heard about an international organisation called WWOOF (Willing Workers On Organic Farms). WWOOF provides food and accommodation for volunteer members in exchange for five or six hours of work. Being a solo traveller with rapidly dwindling funds I thought it sounded like an excellent idea and joined up.

The first farm I stayed on was like something out of a kid's storybook. The farmer was a Frenchman and retired carpenter who had created his own little slice of Provence in northern Tasmania. I found myself eagerly working well beyond the prescribed hours, tending vegetables, fruit trees and chickens. This may have had something to do with the fact that every meal we ate included ingredients that we had toiled to produce. I had never experienced a way of life like this, and as I looked around the farm, the amazing food we were eating and how connected we were to the local community, it became crystal clear to me that this is as good as life gets. I was happy, healthy and loving every second of it, and it all came down to growing a bit of food!

That life-changing experience would eventually lead me to hosting *River Cottage Australia*, sharing with viewers all over Australia and the world the lifestyle that had had such a profound impact on my life. After the program came to an end, I had time to reflect on what fuelled its popularity and managed to bring it down to one core concept: the celebration of people, place and produce, all through the lens of growing food.

I needed to get the message out there, to share this incredible realisation with as many people as possible. So I got writing.

I want this book to be for you, dear reader, what that farm in Tasmania was to me – a window into a life in tune with the seasons, where you grow and cook your own meals and share them with your family and friends. Along with some darn good instructions on how to get there. I want this book to make you feel comfortable to have a go, even if you've never grown or cooked anything in your life. I want this book to be battered and shared, covered in dirt and tomato juice, and turned to whenever you need a bit of inspiration.

So please, get out there and grow something, cook some real food and enjoy the companionship of your nearest and dearest. Trust me, you have nothing to lose and everything to gain.

GROW

Why on earth would you bother growing your own food? It's so readily available at a moment's notice from your nearest supermarket. Heck, you don't even have to leave your house; a quick tap on your phone and the next thing you know, there's a knock on your door and there it is – you didn't even have to break into a sweat! While this ease and convenience seems great on the surface, it closes us off from a meaningful experience that has been part of human existence for as long as we've been putting food in our mouths. I'm not suggesting that you have to shun supermarkets and try to live exclusively off the land, but I believe that through growing our own food, whether that be a little or a lot, we benefit in ways far more numerous than simply putting home-grown produce on the table. And the best part is that anyone can have a go. You don't have to be a green-thumbed master gardener; you don't even need any land – all you need is enthusiasm, patience and a bit of know-how, and you'll be surprised at what you can grow.

My mum is a gun gardener, so you might think I had a bit of a head start, but when I was a kid, being made to garden felt like a punishment as it took me away from my precious video games. It meant spending my school holidays shovelling mountains of mulch that Mum used to transform a stony paddock into a show-garden masterpiece. Classic kid, I had little appreciation for what she was doing at the time, but luckily she is a patient woman.

Mum preferred growing ornamental plants that would survive and hopefully thrive in the difficult conditions they would face, so the extent of our food growing was a lone orange tree. It struggled for years until it finally came good and started to provide us with buckets of the most amazing oranges every single year. I guess that was the first time I realised that the flavour of stuff you grow at home is a whole lot better than anything you can buy from the shops. To use a bad gardening pun, a small seed had been sown in my mind, though it would be many years before it would take root.

Hosting *River Cottage Australia* gave me the opportunity to meet people from all over Australia who aspired to a productive gardening life with strong ties to their local community, but I was surprised at how few felt they could actually achieve it. The general consensus seemed to be that you could only live like that if you had access to 20 acres of rolling green countryside on the New South Wales south coast. I ruminated on this for a while and realised that the celebration of place, people and produce is not confined to life in the country – that really, people can live a rich life in all three of these things no matter where they are. That light-bulb moment was the impetus for writing this book.

I feel the foundation for all of this is growing your own food in whatever capacity

you can. In my own experience, and the experience of many other gardeners I know, growing food is somewhat of a cure-all for the woes of life. Concerned about global warming and diminishing biodiversity? Grow a diverse garden, sequester some carbon and get a feed while you're doing it! Looking for a way to slow down and be more mindful? Start your own food garden and watch it grow. Want to teach your kids about delayed gratification? Get more movement into your life? Connect with living things in a meaningful way? Know exactly what's going into the food you eat? Get to know your neighbours? The list goes on. And yep, you guessed it: it's time to get yourself a food garden. It really is the magic green bullet, and I can't think of one good reason not to have a crack at growing some of your own food.

Of course, people can always find excuses not to do it – no space, no time, no experience – but all I hear is 'no desire'. If you've always wanted to grow food but have never taken the plunge, then I'll tell you now, there's no time like the present.

On the following pages I've outlined how to get gardening no matter what space you have, how to generate your own garden fertility with nothing but food scraps, how to keep chickens and bees and grow fruit trees, along with a rough guide to growing a stack of popular veggies.

There will always be the occasional setback on your gardening journey; just remember to start small and grow both your garden and experience organically (that's another bad gardening pun right there) and keep your plants fed and watered. Before you know it you'll be boasting to your friends that the food they're eating tastes so good because you grew it. Now get out there and sink those hands into some soil!

GROWING IN POTS

You don't need a farm or even a backyard to have a crack at growing your own food. It's amazing what you can grow in pots on a sunny windowsill or in a courtyard. While you won't be able to grow enough to ditch the supermarket, you will certainly be able to liven up your meals and your living space.

A small container-based garden is the perfect place to start your food-growing adventure – you don't need big veggie beds and you don't really need any tools. It will help you to build your skills as a gardener without committing huge amounts of time or resources.

A container garden will also reduce your food waste, as when you have ingredients like herbs and leafy greens on hand, you only pick what you need, rather than buying a whole bunch for a few leaves and watching the rest turn into a green sludge in your crisper drawer.

POSITION

When it comes to choosing a place to grow food, not all spots are created equal. The number one factor to take into account is the amount of direct sunlight your plants will receive. Most food plants need at least 6 hours of direct sunlight a day to thrive, which means that south-facing windowsill or courtyard with a view to your neighbour's high fence is out. The ideal spot for growing faces roughly between north and south, as this allows for plenty of gentle, year-round sun. West-facing positions can get blazing hot in summer; you can get away with exposing your plants to this intense sunlight, but you'll have to be vigilant about watering them. If you don't have a spot that gets enough sunlight, an alternative is to find (or start!) a local community garden instead.

WHAT YOU'LL NEED

Pots or containers for your plants

Any size that you can fit in your space will do the trick, but I'd recommend they're at least 15 cm deep and have holes in the bottom for drainage. I also like to add a thin layer of coarse gravel to the bottom of my pots to ensure excess water can drain away freely. Larger plants like tomatoes or chillies are best planted by themselves in a bigger pot, while herbs and greens can be grown solo in smaller pots or together in larger pots. Just remember that space, water and nutrients are limited when growing in pots, so don't overcrowd your plants! It's also a good idea to sit the pots in a tray or saucer so that any runoff after watering is safely captured, especially if you're pots are on a windowsill. You don't want dirty water trickling down the wall onto your nice carpet.

Potting mix

When you're growing on this micro scale it's best to use a high-quality potting mix. The medium that you choose to grow your plants in will have a huge impact on their health. Using regular soil can lead to disease and pest problems, so seek out a potting mix (preferably organic) that is specifically designed for growing plants in containers and has been enriched with compost or manures rather than slow-release chemicals. It's important not to skimp on this one – buy the best potting mix you can find as your plants will later embody it.

Tools

The great thing about growing in containers is that you really don't need any tools. A small watering can that produces a fine stream will cover both your watering needs and liquid fertiliser application. A small hand-pump spray mister is also handy for keeping plants fresh and happy during the heat of summer, especially in houses where air-conditioning is used.

Suitable plants

Herbs This is the main crop I focus on for pot growing, especially if they are in or near the kitchen. Herbs like chives, rosemary, thyme and oregano are perfect for beginners as they are robust and forgiving for those who haven't quite developed their green thumbs. Once you're feeling a little more confident, try planting some parsley, basil and coriander.

Cut-and-come-again greens What on earth are these, you ask? Greens that grow without forming a single head. Think rocket, not iceberg lettuce. These kinds of greens are perfect for growing in containers because they are not heavy feeders and don't mind being a little crowded, plus there is a world of difference between the quality of greens you buy from the shops and ones that you harvest moments before eating them. Look for varieties like land cress, rocket, spinach, loose-leaf lettuces, mustard, mizuna, kale and rainbow chard.

Spring onions These are great for adding a little punch to your cooking, and perfect for growing in small containers as they have a very shallow root system and can be grown very densely. You can even grow your own spring onions by planting the leftover roots from bunches you have bought!

Chillies I am a chilli fiend, so I love having a few varieties on hand to pick and add to my cooking. Chillies offer amazing flavour bang for your space buck, and one or two plants can keep even the most die-hard chilli nut stocked up for most of the year. They will need a decent-sized pot to thrive – at least 30 cm deep with a diameter of 30 cm or more. Look for varieties that produce small fruit and have a compact, bushy tendency.

Sprouts and microgreens The ultimate small-space crop, these take up minimal space, are very portable, return a yield quickly, and are delicious and nutrient dense. See page 20 for more information on how to grow your own.

MAINTENANCE

When growing in small containers you have to be very conscious of the limited supply of the two things (other than sunshine) a plant needs to survive: food and water. Staying on top of your watering is extra important if you're growing your plants on a sunny windowsill as indoor environments tend to have low humidity, and plants and potting mixes can dry out very quickly. As a rule of thumb, give your plants a little water every other day. The best test is to push your finger down into the soil – if it feels moist 2 cm below the surface, there is adequate water.

Mineral salts can also accumulate over time, which can have an adverse effect on the health of your plants. To mitigate this, give them a really good soaking once a month – this will flush out any harmful build up.

To make sure your plants are well fed, it's essential to start with a potting mixture that has been enriched with compost or worm castings. Once your plants are in the soil, a fortnightly application of organic liquid seaweed fertiliser should be enough to satisfy their growing needs.

If your plants are annuals and will only last for a season, such as greens, after you do your final harvest and remove the plant, top up the container with some compost or worm castings before planting the next crop to replenish the nutrients available to your plants. If your plants are perennial, like many herbs, repot your plants into fresh potting mix every year to ensure they stay healthy and strong.

GROW YOUR OWN
SPROUTS &
MICROGREENS

Just because you don't have access to your own patch of dirt doesn't mean that you can't grow your own delicious plants, using only a tiny sliver of space. Seeds are chock-a-block with nutritional value, containing everything a plant needs to begin growing, and the best way to unlock all that goodness for us to eat is to start the germination process. This can be done in one of two ways: by sprouting or by growing microgreens. Both are straightforward, take up hardly any space, and will add colour, texture and nutrients to your diet.

The major difference between sprouts and microgreens is that sprouts are germinated in a vessel by repeatedly rinsing with water, and are consumed seed, sprout and all, while microgreens are germinated in a seed-raising mix and cut off at the soil level for consumption after the first two to four leaves appear.

I'm going to show you how to make your own sprouting and microgreen set-ups using simple materials you'll most likely have at hand, though if you prefer you can buy kits for either from good garden retailers.

SPROUTS

WHAT YOU'LL NEED

Seeds The seed of almost any edible plant variety can be used for sprouting, but if you're just starting out, try classics like radish, lentils, broccoli, alfalfa, mung beans, mustard and chickpeas. For best results, purchase organic, untreated sprouting seed mixes from good seed retailers.

A wide-mouth glass jar I like to use old peanut butter jars, which have a capacity of about 400 g. Give the jar a good clean in soapy water before you start.

A clean, stainless steel sieve For straining the soaking liquid.

Breathable, natural fabric I use old 100% cotton t-shirts, but cheesecloth will work just fine too. Cut the fabric to a size slightly larger than the top of the jar.

A rubber band To secure the fabric to the jar.

A bowl To rest the jar in.

A clean tea towel To air-dry the sprouts.

WHAT TO DO

1 Place 1 tablespoon of your desired seeds in a jar and cover them with plenty of cool water. Leave the jar on a benchtop, out of the sun, and let the seeds soak for at least 8 hours. I usually prepare mine in the evening and let them soak overnight.

2 Place a clean stainless steel sieve over the top of the jar. Tip the jar upside down and drain out all the liquid, keeping the seeds in the jar. Add some more cool water to the jar and give it a good swish around to rinse the seeds, then drain off this water too, keeping the sieve over the jar opening.

3 Place the fabric cover on the jar and secure it with a rubber band, then place the jar upside down in a bowl so that it sits on an angle, draining any excess liquid into the bowl. Leave the bowl and jar at room temperature out of direct sunlight. Repeat the rinsing and draining process twice daily until your sprouts are ready. For most seeds this will take 3–7 days.

4 Take the fabric off the jar and spread the sprouts onto a clean tea towel to air-dry for 30 minutes or so. Transfer to an airtight container and pop them in the fridge, where they'll keep for up to a week.

MICROGREENS

WHAT YOU'LL NEED

A small tray Around 5 cm deep is fine. I like to use the punnets that strawberries come in or 2 litre milk cartons cut in half from top to bottom.

Seed-raising mix Look for this at your local garden centre; it's perfectly formulated for germinating seeds.

Seeds As with sprouts, you can use the seeds of pretty much any edible plant for growing microgreens. Some easy-to-grow options are basil, beetroot, broccoli, coriander, mustard, parsley, sunflowers, peas, radish, rocket and sorrel. Be sure to purchase organic untreated seeds from a quality seed retailer.

Organic liquid fertiliser I like to use a dilution of a seaweed-derived fertiliser to make sure the growing microgreens are packed with nutrients.

WHAT TO DO

1 Line the base of your tray with a piece of paper to stop any soil from escaping, then fill it with around 3 cm of seed-raising mix.

2 Spread a generous layer of seeds evenly over the top of the soil mix, then gently pat them down into the soil.

3 Give the seeds a water using a fine spray – it's essential that the seed-raising mix is kept moist until the seeds germinate. Continue watering regularly as the plants grow, using the fine spray. Every couple of days, dilute some organic liquid fertiliser (using the ratio of 50 parts water to 1 part fertiliser, or just a few drops in 200 ml or so of water) and give the soil and germinating seeds a good misting. This will make sure your microgreens grow strongly and are packed with nutrition.

4 Your microgreens are ready to harvest when the second set of leaves appear. Use a sharp pair of scissors to cut them just above the soil level. For optimum nutrition and freshness, harvest them right before you're ready to use them.

MAKE A
WICKING BED

One of the biggest traps first-time gardeners fall into is not watering their plants enough, especially when growing in containers during the heat of summer. We all have busy lives that take us away from our gardens and it's easy to miss a watering or two, but unfortunately this can lead to our precious plants becoming stressed, or, gasp, dying. If this story sounds familiar, let me introduce you to the wonderful world of wicking beds.

A wicking bed is a self-contained growing system that essentially functions as a giant self-watering pot, where the soil is watered from underneath rather than from above. I know, it sounds a bit like magic, but it works through a simple capillary action. In the bottom of the container is a reservoir of water that keeps the soil and the plant roots above it moist. The reservoir is topped up via a PVC pipe that sticks out the top of the bed and any excess water runs out of a drainage hole that's level with the top of the reservoir.

Wicking beds can come in a whole range of different shapes and sizes, but I'm going to show you how to make a very simple one that's perfect for growing shallow-rooted plants like lettuce, leafy greens and herbs. This is a small bed, though you can make wicking beds much larger, sturdier and more permanent. If that's what you're after, a quick search online will uncover myriad designs and advice to help you build your beds.

WHAT YOU'LL NEED

A drill For drilling drainage holes into the PVC pipe and for the overflow into the boxes.

45 cm length of 50 mm PVC pipe If you're lucky you might have a bit of this lying around, otherwise they are available from hardware or plumbing supply stores.

A polystyrene box that doesn't have any holes in the bottom Ask around at your local greengrocer or supermarket; they generally have truckloads of these and are more than happy for someone to take a few off their hands. If you're looking for something a little sturdier, any solid plastic tub of a similar size (without drainage holes) will do the job.

An aggregate Try scoria, bluestone or, in my case, smashed up old terracotta roof tiles.

An old t-shirt or some weed matting This is to keep the aggregate and soil separate, while allowing water to pass through. When my old t-shirts start to get threadbare I chuck them in the shed and save them for lining wicking beds, or I cut them up and use them to tie tomatoes to their stakes.

Good-quality soil or potting mix Preferably organic and the best you can afford.

WHAT TO DO

1 With your drill, make a series of 6–8 holes in the first 10 cm of one end of the PVC pipe.

2 Place the pipe, drilled end down, vertically in one corner of your polystyrene box, then fill the bottom third of the box with the aggregate. Give the pipe a bit of a wiggle to ensure it is sitting flush with the bottom of the box.

3 Drill a 1 cm hole in the side of the box, level with the top of the aggregate.

4 Lay the t-shirt or matting on top of the aggregate so that it extends to all four sides of the box.

5 Place your soil on top, then fill the reservoir using the PVC pipe until water starts to flow out the drainage hole.

6 Plant your seedlings in the soil.

TIPS

> Make sure that you keep the level in your reservoir topped up by watering it once a week and filling until water starts to come out of the overflow.

> Give the reservoir a good flush every 12 months by watering the beds until water flows out of the overflow for a good couple of minutes. A large rainfall event will also do this for you.

> Add compost or worm castings to the soil in between plantings to make sure your plants have access to plenty of nutrients. Looked after properly, a wicking bed should last indefinitely.

SET UP A
BOKASHI

Living in a home without any outdoor space can present a challenge when it comes to dealing with food scraps. You're hardly likely to set up a compost heap in the spare bedroom and a worm farm takes up precious real estate if you're pressed for space. But don't despair, there is a solution that's specifically designed for use indoors. Bokashi, which translates from Japanese to 'fermented organic material', is not just a cool-sounding word, it is a means to deal with kitchen scraps using a process of anaerobic fermentation.

The system, which was invented by Japanese soil scientist Dr Teruo Higa, uses a mixture of microorganisms to ferment food scraps in the anaerobic environment of a sealed bucket over a period of around 2 weeks, producing a 'pickled' soil conditioner as well as a nutritious liquid that can be diluted in water to feed plants (30 ml in a 9-litre watering can). The advantages of the bokashi system are that they are super easy to use, totally self contained, don't smell, don't need turning and can deal with all your household food scraps.

However, it's not a perfect system. The major drawback is that the pickled material isn't a finished soil and needs to be dug into the ground, fed to worms or composted further after the fermentation period is complete. This can be challenging if you live in an apartment because the whole reason for using a bokashi system is that you don't have a compost or worm farm.

To get around this, why not reach out to a community garden or a friend with a worm farm or compost heap, and offer the fermented material to them – or you could take it to your local park and bury it near your favourite tree to give it a feed. Another alternative is to use your bokashi mix in pots or planters. You can fill them with one-third potting mix, then add one-third bokashi mixture and mix the two together, top with another one-third potting mix and leave it for 2 weeks before planting into the pots.

Bokashi buckets and bran (which contains the microorganisms needed for the process) are generally sold as pre-made kits and can be purchased from gardening or hardware stores, but if you're feeling like getting your DIY on, just do a quick search online and you will be making your own bokashi bucket and bran in no time.

WHAT YOU'LL NEED

A bokashi bucket Available from gardening stores or online

Bokashi bran A dry material inoculated with the necessary microorganisms

A potato masher For pushing down your scraps

WHAT CAN YOU PUT IN IT?

Pretty much any food scraps, including meat and dairy

Coffee grinds

Wilted flowers

Tissues

WHAT NOT TO PUT IN IT?

Liquids

Paper

Large bones

WHAT TO DO

1 Open the bucket and add a 3–4 cm layer of scraps to the grate in the bottom of the bucket.

2 Add the bokashi bran in the ratio of 1 tablespoon of bran to every cup of food scraps, though it's always better to err on the side of adding too much bran rather than too little, especially when dealing with high protein scraps like meat and dairy.

3 Use a potato masher to push down the food scraps to force out any air pockets.

4 Replace the lid, ensuring that it's on tight. Repeat whenever you have food scraps to dispose of.

5 Drain the liquid from the reservoir a few times a week.

6 Once full, leave the bucket to ferment for 2 weeks.

7 When ready, the scraps will still look relatively intact. They can now be dug into the soil, fed to a worm farm or added to a compost heap.

TIPS

> Make sure you squash down the scraps and keep the lid airtight.

> Chop up any bulky scraps to speed up the process.

> Drain the liquid regularly.

> Make sure you use enough of the bokashi bran.

GROWING IN A BACKYARD

A bit of grass, a Hills Hoist, a little garden shed, maybe a lemon tree. If this scene sounds familiar, then you're probably part of the 70 per cent of Australians who live in a free-standing house with some sort of yard. If that's the case, and you're keen to try your hand at growing food, you're in luck because with all that space there's a whole lot of food growing you can do!

Forget about vast swathes of sterile lawn. If you take the plunge and turn over some (or all!) of your back (or front!) yard to growing food, your yard will be transformed into a vibrant ecosystem, which will provide you with fresh food and become a haven for all manner of colour and life. It's not going to be a piece of cake. There will be sweat, tears and a whole lot of dedication required, but if you start small, listen to your plants and get composting, then a cornucopia of gardening goodness awaits.

CHOOSE A POSITION

Fruiting plants (tomatoes, pumpkins, zucchini) need around 6 hours of direct sunlight a day, so you'll need to pick a spot that ticks that box. If you don't have anywhere that gets that much light, you can still have a crack at growing things like lettuce, leafy greens and herbs in areas that receive at least a couple of hours of direct sunlight daily.

Slope is another thing to consider when siting your garden. In a perfect world, your garden would slope gently to the north so that all your plants could share ample sunshine, but there's still hope if you have a garden that's dead flat or steeply sloping. If your garden is flat, build your beds up a little to assist with drainage when there's a big downpour, and if your garden is on a slope, you can build terraced beds to give you some flat spots for planting.

TEND TO YOUR SOIL

This may seem obvious, but just because you've got a patch of dirt to turn over to a veggie garden doesn't mean your soil is going to be capable of growing healthy, nutritious food. Soils are made up of three main components: sand, clay and silt, with vegetables preferring a rich balance of all three. If you live somewhere that has sand- or clay-heavy soil, growing vegetables will be a challenge but you can give your garden a fighting chance by adding as much compost and organic matter as you can get your hands on, or by building raised beds and bringing in good soil specifically for growing veggies. Over time, as you continue to add organic matter, your soil will improve.

It's also important to test your soil's pH, which is a measure of how acidic it is. Most veggies do well in a very slightly acidic soil with a pH between 6.0 and 7.0. Testing is straightforward, and kits are readily available from garden centres or hardware stores.

If you live in a high-density urban area, near an industrial area or in a suburb that used to be home to industry, it's definitely worth getting your soil tested for heavy-metal contamination. The last thing you want to do is grow fresh food that is laced with poisonous heavy metals and then feed it to your family. Macquarie University offers a donation-based testing service that is available in all Australian states and territories. Head over to their website (research.science.mq.edu.au/vegesafe) to learn more.

CHOOSE A WATERING SYSTEM

Growing in soil gives you a much better buffer against hot, dry weather than growing in containers, although it's not without its challenges. Watering with a hose or watering can is the most water-efficient way to hydrate your garden but it can be very time consuming if you have a large garden and need to water every day in the heat of summer. Overhead sprinklers are a cheap way to cover a lot of ground, but they are terribly inefficient, spraying water all over the garden. The best way to keep your veggies watered is to invest time and money into installing some drip irrigation. The pipes lie on the soil along your garden beds and drip a steady stream of water straight onto the soil, meaning there is minimal loss from evaporation and wind drift. Add a timer and watering becomes a breeze, although I still like to walk around with the hose every couple of days so I can have a good look at my plants.

DON'T FORGET TO MULCH

Mulching is an efficient way of keeping your soil moist and your plants happy. It involves spreading weed- and seed-free plant material like straw or hay over the bare soil of your garden. This layer of insulation keeps moisture in and excessive heat out; in addition, as it decomposes it enriches your soil with extra organic matter. Just make sure you source mulch that is weed free, otherwise you might inadvertently introduce new weeds into your garden beds.

TURN YOUR GRASS INTO GARDEN

When was the last time you went out to your lawn and picked yourself some lunch? Unless you happen to be a sheep, I bet the answer is never! We seem to have a misguided obsession with expanses of boring green grass, which takes nearly as much effort to maintain as growing vegetables, but gives us nothing in return. The fact that we live on such a dry continent makes the pursuit of the perfect lawn seem even more futile. I've even seen people resort to laying astro turf around their homes for that green-grass effect without any of the effort. What have we come to? Now, I'm not totally anti-lawn – I always have a small patch for the kids and dog to play on, or so that I can put up a tent for any impromptu guests – but for me it's garden first, grass second. If you feel the same way and would like to turn some of your grass into an abundant veggie patch, here's how to do it.

PICK YOUR TIME OF YEAR

While technically you could dig a garden bed any time of the year, you're much better waiting for a bit of cooler weather. Nothing drains enthusiasm faster than sweating on the end of a shovel on a blasting hot day.

PICK YOUR SPOT

Remember, you'll need somewhere with plenty of sunshine and shelter from winds, ideally with a gentle slope. If you're just starting out I recommend a small garden to begin with; say, no bigger than 10 square metres. Once you get the hang of looking after that, you can always expand your garden later.

MARK OUT YOUR BEDS

Take a shovel and dig around the edges of your bed so that it's clearly defined.

GET RID OF THE GRASS

There are a couple of ways you can do this, depending on how much time you have and what type of grass it is. If you're the 'minimum effort, maximum result' type you can layer cardboard thickly onto the grass and weigh it down so it doesn't blow away. The cardboard will stop sunlight reaching the grass, causing it to wither and die over a couple of weeks. This method is suitable for most types of grass, except for more vigorous running grasses like Kikuyu. Once the grass has died off, remove the cardboard and get ready to dig your beds.

If you're the 'Let's get it done today!' type, then grab a mattock or shovel and dig that grass out the old-fashioned way. This is more labour intensive, but the advantage is that you can start and finish on the same day. Use the mattock to chip out the grass, shaking excess soil away from the roots. If the grass is a non-running type and has no seed heads, you can chuck it straight into your compost.

AERATE THE SOIL

Aerating the soil makes it easy for plant roots to spread and for the soil to hold moisture. Once all of the grass is removed, starting with one edge, drive a garden fork down into the soil then lean it right back towards you to lift and break up the soil. Work sideways in a line, then take a step or two back and start a new line, being careful not to stand on and compress any of your newly aerated soil.

ADD SOME ORGANIC MATTER

Give your soil a bit of a nutritional boost by adding some organic matter like compost or well-rotted manure. A couple of shovel loads per square metre will do the trick, scattered evenly around your beds. Rake the compost in, breaking up any clumps of soil that survived the forking. If you're planting seeds you'll want the soil to be as finely raked as possible, but if you're planting seedlings a few little clumps here and there won't hurt.

MARK YOUR PATHS

For any beds wider than 1.2 metres you'll need to lay some paths so you can access the whole bed without walking on it and compressing the soil. Plan your paths so you don't have to reach more than 50 cm or so into the bed to plant, weed, mulch, etc. I make my paths about a shovel width by running a shovel flattish along the ground and then scooping any loose soil into the beds. You can cover your paths with sawdust or woodchips if you have some handy, but I find that regular foot traffic and pulling weeds as you see them is enough to keep the paths clear.

TIME TO PLANT!

When it comes to choosing what to put into your newly created beds, it's worth taking a few things into consideration. Firstly, it's important to make sure you choose the right plants for your climate and the time of year. Have a look at the planting guide starting on page 70 to get an idea of what works. Secondly, it's important to plant food that you actually want to eat! It's all very well to plant ten different varieties of lettuce, but if you're not really a salad person, you're wasting your precious time and space.

CREATE A
NO-DIG GARDEN

Somewhere between growing food in containers and planting veggies in the ground lies a very practical alternative: the no-dig garden. It's going to cost you a little more than just planting in the ground, but on the plus side it will provide plenty of food for your growing plants and has excellent moisture retention compared with growing in containers. It's essentially a raised bed made with layers of organic materials that can be placed straight over your lawn or even over concrete, and then planted directly into. No digging required.

No-dig gardens were pioneered by Sydney woman Esther Deans in the 1970s as a response to her unworkable clay soils. In the process she created a vegetable- and flower-growing paradise! No-dig gardens are perfect for renters because you can grow your own food without digging up the landlord's precious lawn, and they also have the added benefit of improving the soil underneath them without needing to dig it up. If this sounds like your idea of gardening, here's what you'll need.

WHAT YOU'LL NEED

Something to make the bed borders from I like to use bales of weed-free straw because they're relatively cheap, they're easy to install, and as they break down they feed your garden. If you're after something more permanent, you can construct a border using timber, bricks or rocks, building the border up to a height of around 30 cm if you're placing the bed over soil, or 50 cm if you're placing it over concrete.

Cardboard or coarse gravel I like to thickly layer cardboard in the bottom of the no-dig bed to supress any grass growing up through your veggies. If you're building your beds over a hard surface like concrete, replace this with coarse gravel to provide drainage.

Straw One of the layers for your no-dig beds, this provides drainage and keeps your beds light and friable.

Well-rotted cow manure Another layer for your beds, this will provide ample food for your growing plants.

A compost-enriched veggie-growing mix This is the final layer for your beds and is available from most landscape-supply businesses.

Optional extras Blood and bone, lime or pelletised chook manure. This can be lightly sprinkled over every couple of layers to turbocharge your beds.

Mulch To protect the soil.

WHAT TO DO

1 Choose a position that is nice and sheltered from the wind and gets ample sunlight, then construct the border. Make sure your beds are no wider than 1.5 metres as you'll need to be able to reach the centre without standing in the beds. Lay your cardboard over the base of the bed, a couple of layers deep.

2 Give your cardboard a good soaking with the hose so that it's completely wet.

3 Add a 10 cm layer of straw on top of the cardboard and water it in.

4 Top the straw with a layer of cow manure and water it in.

5 Next, add a layer of the veggie-growing mix and water it in.

6 Repeat this layering until the bed is roughly level with the top of the border or even bulging a little higher. The soil level will naturally drop as the beds mature.

7 Plant into your beds (see Tips).

8 Give everything a good watering in and then mulch around your plants. Over time the soil level will drop – you can fix this by adding fresh layers in between plantings.

TIPS

> If you don't mind things looking a little messier in the garden, you can skip the border of straw bales altogether and just build the layers freeform on the ground.

> Use these beds in spots that have poor soil. You'll be able to grow veggies immediately and over time all that organic material will enrich the poor soil underneath.

> You can grow pretty much anything in a no-dig garden; just make sure you're planting at the right time of year for your climate.

> No-dig gardens are great for rentals. You can build them directly on top of the lawn, then when it comes time to move out, just spread the materials over the lawn and mow them in. You'll be doing your landlord's lawn a favour by giving it a big feed!

MAKE A
WORM FARM

Worms are a gardener's best friend; they're very easy to keep, they'll eat up a good chunk of your kitchen scraps, and in return they offer you worm castings and worm wee, both of which will work wonders for your plants. Although worms are pretty low maintenance, they do have a few living requirements in order to thrive. They like to live at temperatures between 18°C and 24°C, so in summer you'll need a cool spot that's out of direct sunlight and in winter you'll need a spot that gets a bit of sun, so they can stay nice and warm. Worms will deal with most types of kitchen scraps as well as a bit of damp cardboard and newspaper, but it's best to avoid feeding them overly acidic foods like onion, garlic and citrus. It's also best to exclude animal products like meat and dairy as they can turn rancid and attract unwanted pests. You also want your worms living in a home where it is easy to collect the castings and worm wee. Worm farms are readily available at garden centres and hardware shops, although it's also a piece of cake and super cheap to make your own.

WHAT YOU'LL NEED

A screwdriver or similar For making drain holes.

Two polystyrene boxes that are the same size You'll need to find the type that doesn't have any holes in the bottom and has a lid. Broccoli boxes are perfect, so ask your local supermarket or greengrocer if they have any out the back. In my experience they are always glad to get rid of them!

A few crates or a stack of bricks to sit your worm farm on You'll need your worm farm to be elevated a little, so you can easily collect the worm wee as they make it.

An old bit of mesh It needs to be large enough to line the base of the top box so the worm castings don't fall into the bottom box.

A few handfuls of straw or shredded newspaper (or a combination) This is your bedding material.

Watering can For dampening the bedding material.

Worm starter pack You can buy these from garden centres and hardware shops, or if you have a friend whose worm farm is pumping, ask if they can spare a couple of big handfuls.

An old cotton t-shirt To lay on top of the worms, the bedding and the food to keep everything cool and damp.

A jar For collecting the worm wee.

WHAT TO DO

1 Use the screwdriver or something similar to punch some holes in a 5 cm cluster at one end of the box that will be the bottom storey of your worm farm. This is so the worm wee can drain into your collection jar.

2 Place the bottom box on its stand.

3 Next, punch a series of holes all over the bottom of the other box, which will become the second storey of your worm farm. This is so the worm wee can drain from the top box to the bottom box where it can be collected.

4 Lay the mesh over the bottom of the second storey box so that it covers the base entirely.

5 Add your bedding material to the lined box and place it on top of the first box. Use a watering can to dampen it.

6 Add your worms, spreading them out over the bedding.

7 Place the t-shirt over the worms and dampen it with a watering can, then pop the lid on the box. I like to let my worms settle in for a day or so before starting to feed them, and always start feeding them slowly. Worms will eat roughly their own body weight in a day, but it's always better to underfeed them a little until you get

the hang of how much your worm farm can handle. When it's time to feed them, open the lid, peel back the t-shirt and scatter the food scraps evenly over the bedding. Replace the t-shirt and put the lid back on.

8 Place the jar underneath the drainage holes to collect the worm wee.

TIPS

> Don't let your worm farm dry out in summer; dampen a little with a watering can if it looks a little dry.

> Chop up your food scraps a little to make it easier for your worms to eat.

> To harvest your worm castings, feed in one end of the box for a week to attract the worms, then scoop out the castings from the opposite end.

> Use worm castings as you would compost, as a top dressing around your plants or raked into garden beds.

> Use worm wee as a liquid fertiliser, diluted 1 part worm wee to 10 parts water.

> Don't overfeed your worms!

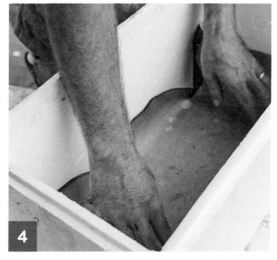

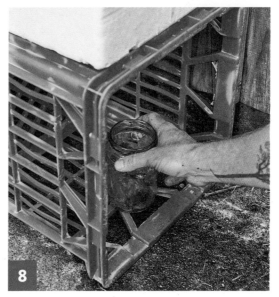

COMPOSTING 101

There is something magical about composting. You pile all your kitchen scraps into a bin and months later, through the power of microbes, they're transformed into rich black soil, which can work miracles in the garden. If you've tried your hand at composting before, only to end up with a smelly mess that attracted mice and upset your neighbours, don't be discouraged – with a little more know-how you'll be churning out the sweet stuff in no time. Getting the basics of composting is super simple: it's all about getting the right balance of green (nitrogenous) materials, brown (carbonaceous) materials, water and oxygen right. It might sound a little daunting, but microbes do all the heavy lifting. You just have to provide the right conditions.

CHOOSE A SYSTEM

There's more than one way to make compost, so before you start you'll need to choose a system. The three basic setups are a manufactured bin, a tumbler and homemade composting bays.

A bin is a great way to get started and is relatively contained, but they can be difficult to aerate so it's worth investing in a spiral aerator to keep your compost nice and oxygenated. One modification that I would recommend is to cover the base with rodent mesh to stop rats and mice burrowing up into your compost.

Tumblers are a good choice if you don't generate very much kitchen waste. They are totally contained and easily aerated when not overfilled.

Homemade composting bays are a great solution if you've got plenty of space and aren't too close to your neighbours. They're cheap to build (three pallets and some corrugated iron will do the trick) and can take loads of kitchen scraps. The major setback is that they are difficult to make fully enclosed and can attract pests.

WHAT TO PUT IN IT?

Compostable materials can be split into two main categories: greens and browns. For happy compost, I use the ratio of one bucket of greens to one bucket of browns.

GREEN MATERIALS INCLUDE:

> Fruit and vegetable scraps

> Coffee grounds

> Old plants that you've pulled out from the veggie patch

> Animal manure (except cat or dog)

> Seaweed

> Eggshells

> Non-invasive weeds that haven't set seed

BROWN MATERIALS INCLUDE:

> Egg cartons

> Torn-up cardboard boxes

> Tissues

> Dry grass clippings

> Dried-up flowers

> Shredded, non-glossy paper

> Dried leaves

WHAT TO DO

Keep adding equal parts brown and green materials to your compost, giving it a good aerate every week or so. Once your compost bin is full, let it mature for a couple of months before using it. (Ideally, you'll have at least two bins so you can be filling one as the other one matures.) You can empty the bin and spread the compost around the garden all at once or leave it in the bin and use it as required.

TROUBLESHOOTING

Compost stinks: Lack of oxygen. Give your pile a good turn and incorporate a little more brown material.

Looks too dry: Lack of moisture. Dampen the compost with some water and incorporate some more green material.

Looks too wet: Too much green material. Incorporate some more brown material.

Full of bugs: Don't stress, bugs will be present in a healthy compost. They all play a role in the decomposition process and the soil-food web.

GROWING FRUIT TREES

No home farm would be truly complete without a fruit tree or two to supplement the veggie crops. The saying goes that the best time to plant your fruit trees was yesterday, because, unlike fast-growing vegetables, planting fruit trees is an act of optimism as they can take years to reward your stewardship with a harvest. Ideally, you should plant your trees directly in the soil where they will grow for decades to come, but if you're living in a rental property or have a small, sunny courtyard, you can still grow fruit trees. Rather than planting them in the soil, you can grow dwarf varieties in large pots, moving them as required.

There are thousands of varieties of fruit trees out there, but they all share a few simple requirements. Almost all fruit trees like to grow in full sun, so when you're picking out where to put them, make sure they'll get around 8 hours of summer sun a day. Fruit trees hate getting bashed around by the weather, so in addition to picking a sunny spot, make sure you find a position where they won't get blasted by strong winds.

Fruit trees also need plenty of room to grow. If you have a tiny backyard, growing a couple of standard avocado trees that could grow up to 12 metres tall isn't such a crash-hot idea, so before you buy your trees, ask your local nursery how big they'll get and make sure you have enough room for them to thrive.

Finally, fruit trees absolutely love free-draining soil, so if your soil has too much clay in it your trees will get wet feet and their health will suffer. If you do have clay-dominant soil, make sure you dig as large a hole as possible when planting your fruit trees – much bigger than the pot the tree comes in – and fill it with some purchased high-quality soil, compost and well-rotted manure before planting your tree.

To give a fruit tree the best head start, dig a nice big hole – twice as deep and twice as wide as the pot the tree comes in – and load it full of well-rotted compost. Then plant the young fruit tree straight into that. Finally, surround your tree with a deep mulch that runs all the way out to the tree's drip line (basically the circumference of the canopy, which mirrors the thirsty roots underneath the soil). Make sure the mulch doesn't come into direct contact with the tree's trunk, otherwise you run the risk of excess moisture being trapped around the trunk, which can lead to decay and pest attack.

It is essential to take good care of your fruit trees during the first couple of years as they become established, but once they have plunged their roots deep into the soil they tend to be pretty hardy. With judicious watering and feeding they will provide you (and possibly your children and grandchildren) with a harvest of delicious abundance for many years to come.

Here's a list of some popular fruit trees with a little information on how to grow them.

APPLE

> **Common varieties:** Fuji, Cox's Orange Pippin, Granny Smith, Gala

> **Climate:** Cold and temperate; low-chill varieties can be grown in the subtropics

> **Size:** Up to 8 metres

> **Self fertile?** No, you'll need at least two trees

> **When to plant:** Plant bare-rooted trees in winter

> **When to feed:** Spring, summer and autumn

> **When to water:** In summer, one deep watering a week

> **How long to first harvest:** 3–6 years

AVOCADO

> **Common varieties:** Reed, Hass (A types) and Bacon, Fuerte (B types)

> **Climate:** Tropical, subtropical, temperate – just pick the right variety

> **Size:** Up to 12 metres, Dwarf varieties up to 4 metres

> **Self fertile?** No, for best results you'll need both an A flowering and B flowering plant

> **When to plant:** Spring

> **When to feed:** Late spring, summer and again in early autumn

> **When to water:** Every week over summer

> **How long to first harvest:** 3–4 years

FIG

> **Common varieties:** Black Genoa, Brown Turkey, White Genoa

> **Climate:** Subtropical, temperate

> **Size:** Up to 10 metres

> **Self fertile?** Yes, except for a few less common varieties

> **When to plant:** Autumn or winter

> **When to feed:** Autumn

> **When to water:** Early spring and a little over summer during dry years

> **How long to first harvest:** 1–2 years

LEMON

> **Common varieties:** Eureka, Lisbon, Meyer

> **Climate:** Temperate, frost sensitive

> **Size:** Up to 8 metres

> **Self fertile?** Yes

> **When to plant:** Late winter/early spring

> **When to feed:** Late summer, late winter

> **When to water:** Every week over summer

> **How long to first harvest:** 3–5 years

MULBERRY

> **Common varieties:** White Shahtoot, Hicks Fancy, Black English

> **Climate:** Cold, subtropical, temperate

> **Size:** Up to 20 metres

> **Self fertile?** Yes

> **When to plant:** Spring

> **When to feed:** Spring and autumn

> **When to water:** Every week or so in summer

> **How long to first harvest:** 2–3 years

OLIVE

> **Common varieties:** Kalamata, Frantoio, Manzanillo

> **Climate:** Temperate – olives like a cool winter and a hot, dry summer

> **Size:** Up to 10 metres

> **Self fertile?** Yes

> **When to plant:** Traditionally autumn, though with adequate water any time is fine

> **When to feed:** Early spring before flowering and again in late summer before harvest

> **When to water:** Regularly while the tree is establishing and then mainly during summer when mature

> **How long to first harvest:** 4–6 years

ORANGE

> **Common varieties:** Valencia, Navel, Blood

> **Climate:** Suitable for most climates

> **Size:** Up to 5 metres

> **Self fertile?** Yes

> **When to plant:** Spring

> **When to feed:** Winter, start and end of summer

> **When to water:** Every week when establishing, every 2–3 weeks when mature

> **How long to first harvest:** 3 years

KEEPING CHOOKS

If you have a decent-sized backyard and you want to produce some incredible, nutritious food that isn't just fruit and veggies, then you can't go past the humble chicken. They'll eat your scraps, they'll chase bugs, they'll produce manure to fertilise your garden and they'll provide you with hours of entertainment, simply watching them go about their daily chores.

On top of all this, they'll provide you with delicious eggs! Getting started with chickens is a piece of cake and with a little daily care, a few hens will provide you with years of eggs and entertainment. Here's a simple guide to what you'll need.

DO YOUR RESEARCH

Before beginning, check with your local council to find out the relevant rules regarding keeping chickens. All of the states and territories in Australia allow chickens to be kept in urban and suburban areas, though there are varying rules around the number you can keep, as well as the type of coop and where it's positioned.

DECIDE HOW MANY CHICKENS YOU NEED

Chickens are social creatures, so you'll need at least two, though I find three is more of a sweet spot. When they're happy and laying, most backyard chooks will provide you with up to six eggs a week. So, if your family goes through two dozen eggs a week, then you'll need about four chooks to meet your egg requirements.

PICK A SPOT

Chickens love to have room to run around, scratch the dirt and chase bugs, and they'll also need shade to shelter under in the summer and nice open patches to sun themselves when it's cold in winter. As a rule of thumb, you'll need to provide at least one square metre for each bird, though I would say that is the absolute minimum and the more space you can give your girls access to, the happier they'll be.

If you have a secure backyard and don't mind inquisitive chickens scratching around (and pooing) everywhere, you can let them wander around your backyard and lock them up in their coop overnight, though for most people (especially if you're growing veggies) a contained run is a much better idea.

To enclose your run, you'll need to drive in posts and surround it with chicken wire that comes up to 1.5 m high. This will keep your chickens in one spot, though it won't keep predators and wild birds out if you want to go away for a couple of days.

Even in urban environments, foxes can be a problem, so to make the ultimate predator-proof enclosure, you'll have to make sure that the chicken wire runs to 50 cm underground to stop them burrowing into the enclosure, as well as making a chicken wire roof that covers the whole run to stop the foxes climbing over the fence and into the pen. A quick search online will yield you loads of designs for predator-proof runs.

BUILD OR BUY A COOP

Chickens need a secure, weather-proof shelter where they can sleep safely, escape the sun and lay their eggs. There are loads of companies out there that sell ready-made, or flat-packed coops, though if you're pretty handy with the tools, you can bang one up for a fraction of the price using recycled materials. As with the run, if you do a quick search online there are thousands of DIY coop designs out there using everything from pallets to old water tanks. A few considerations to keep in mind when building your coop are:

> Your coop should keep out the rain and wind while still having ventilation

> Chickens like to roost off the ground, so provide a couple of perches at different heights that allow at least 30 cm per bird

> Chickens like to lay their eggs in sheltered nooks, so provide nesting boxes, allowing approximately one box for every three birds

> The coop must be totally predator proof

PROVIDE FOOD AND WATER

Keeping chickens comes with responsibility and after providing a secure run and coop, your major concern as a backyard chicken farmer is to make sure they have all the food and water that they need. Chickens need a healthy and varied diet to be happy and lay nutritious eggs, and the foundation of every chicken's diet should be high-quality layer pellets. In addition to pellets, chickens love to eat fruit and vegetable scraps from the kitchen, though avoid feeding them:

> Rhubarb
> Chocolate
> Citrus
> Potato peels
> Anything rancid
  or spoiled

> Avocado
> Onion, garlic, etc.
> Mower clippings
> Anything high in fat
  or salt

If you really want your chickens to thrive you can also grow a range of nutritious plants around your garden to pick and offer them as supplementary feed including:

> Comfrey
> Nasturtiums
> Chickweed

> Wormwood
> Sunflowers
> Mustard greens

Chickens also need a regular supply of calcium to make all those egg shells, which is easily provided by giving them constant access to shell grit. You'll be able to track it down at your local pet supply store.

Of course, in addition to food, chickens need constant access to clean water, with each chicken drinking between 500 ml and 1 litre of water a day depending on the weather. A good-quality water dispenser from your local pet supply store is a relatively small investment and it ensures that your chickens have a constant supply of water.

CHOOSE YOUR BREED

You have your run, your coop and your chickens' food sorted, now all you need is a couple of chooks! There is a dazzling array of chicken breeds out there with every shape, colour and size available. If you've never kept chooks before, I recommend sticking to the classic laying breeds as they'll be relatively low maintenance and provide you with stacks of eggs. A couple of suitable breeds include:

> Rhode Island Red

> Australorp

> Sussex

> Leghorn

> Hybrids like the ISA brown

Avoid the temptation to buy your chickens as chicks, as there are no guarantees that they will be hens, and a backyard full of roosters is a sure-fire way to get your neighbours and the local council offside. I am unfortunately speaking from experience here. When you're ready to buy your chickens, look for a reputable chicken breeder who's selling vaccinated, point-of-lay pullets. These young hens will be in full health and ready to start their laying lives a week or so after you get them home.

Now that you have everything in place, all you have to do is keep your chickens safe, well fed and watered and they will return your care with dozens and dozens of nutrient dense, delicious eggs for ages to come.

KEEPING BEES

Many people find the idea of keeping bees a little intimidating at first – whether it's the fear of getting stung or the thought of managing a colony of tens of thousands of bees. The good news is that bees are relatively happy left to their own devices and all you have to do as a beekeeper is make sure they have access to everything they need and are free from pests and diseases. They don't take up a great deal of space either, and can be kept in most backyards and even on balconies or rooftops. All they need is a nice flat bit of ground big enough for the hive and a clear flight path at the front of the hive so they can go about their business.

If you're keen to keep bees and harvest your own backyard honey I highly recommend getting in touch with your local amateur beekeeping club as they can help you get started. A lifetime of learning goes into becoming a great beekeeper, but here are a few basics to get you under way.

GETTING STARTED

CHOOSE A STYLE OF HIVE

There are loads of different hive designs around, such as Kenyan top-bar, Warre, Flow and Langstroth hives. The most common of these is the Langstroth and it's an easy hive for beginners to learn on. As your skills and confidence increase you may want to explore other types of hives, but for now let's keep it simple. You can pick up a Langstroth starter kit from any beekeeping supplier for under $500, which will include everything you need to build a hive. So what makes up a Langstroth hive?

> **Bottom board:** To elevate the hive off the ground, keeping it dry and well ventilated.

> **Supers:** These are the boxes that house the bees and they come in two different sizes (8 frame and 10 frame). I recommend starting with 8 frame as when the 10-frame supers are loaded with honey they can weigh up to 50 kg and be very difficult for a single person to move.

> **Lid:** Sits on top of the supers to keep the bees sheltered from sun and rain.

> **Frames:** These are the structures bees build honeycomb onto. They come in a variety of depths with or without foundation (a wax or plastic sheet that the bees build upon). To start off, I recommend full-depth frames with wax foundations.

> **Queen excluder:** This is a metal grate that sits between the brood chamber (usually in the bottom super) and the honey supers. It stops the queen from laying brood in supers that are for honey production, so that when it comes to harvesting, the frames are full of honey rather than eggs and baby bees!

INVEST IN SOME EQUIPMENT

I've got a mate who keeps bees without any equipment whatsoever – he inspects his bees totally naked and works his hives with his bare hands. He's a bit of a bee whisperer and if you're a first timer, or even a seasoned beekeeper for that matter, I wouldn't recommend that approach. A few simple bits of kit will make your life as a beekeeper much more pleasurable.

> **Smoker:** Smoke blown into the hive masks the release of stress hormones that alert the bee colony to the presence of an intruder. The smoke also makes the bees think a fire is approaching, and so they gorge themselves on honey, ready to flee the hive and the threat of fire. When the bees are full of honey they are calm and more docile, much like we are after a big meal.

> **Protective clothing:** You can choose how much protection you want here. At a bare minimum I would suggest wearing a light-coloured long-sleeved top, light-coloured pants and closed shoes, with your pants tucked into your socks and your shirt tucked into your pants, along with a veil to protect your face and gloves to protect your hands. (Why light coloured? Because bees have evolved to see bears as a primary threat and dark clothes give a bear-like silhouette. True!) If you're really worried about getting stung, or just want to look super cool like me, you can go for the whole suit with the built-in hood.

> **Hive tool:** A small metal bar used for separating frames that have been joined with wax or propolis, and for assisting in lifting frames out of the hive.

ACQUIRE SOME BEES

Funnily enough, if you want to be a beekeeper you're going to need some bees! Below are a few different ways to acquire them. Whichever method you choose, make sure the bees come from a reputable source and are disease and pest free.

> **Catching a spring swarm:** This is probably not the best idea for a first timer, though once you know how it's surprisingly straightforward. It's a seasonal and free way to populate your hive with bees.

> **Buying a nucleus, AKA a 'nuc':** A nuc is a small colony of bees that comes with all the essentials for starting a hive: bees, brood, food and a queen. This is a great option for beginners and, given the right conditions, the hive will quickly grow into a full colony. Nucs can be purchased from bee breeders for a few hundred dollars.

> **Buying a package of bees:** A package is essentially an artificial swarm consisting of a few thousand worker bees and a queen that's housed in a small cage. Once placed in your hive, the bees will start to build a colony from scratch, which can take a while to establish compared with a nuc. Many beekeepers and bee breeders will offer these for sale, often for around half the price of a nuc.

> **Buying an established hive:** Hives always come up for sale on websites like Gumtree, and you can expect to pay a few hundred dollars for a hive and bees. This is definitely a case of buyer beware. Be sure to thoroughly inspect for any sign of pests or disease – if you don't know what you're looking for, take someone who does.

LEARN HOW TO WORK YOUR BEES

There's too much to know about beekeeping to go into any great detail here. The best advice that I can offer you is to attend a course for beginner beekeepers, join your local beekeeping club, or find another backyard beekeeper who can mentor you. In the meantime, here's a rough rundown of how to inspect your hive.

> Wearing your protective gear, approach the hive calmly from the side or from behind. You don't want to disturb the bees' flight path at the entrance of the hive.

> Blow a little smoke into the entrance of the hive and then remove the lid. Blow a little more smoke down into the top box and use your hive tool to pull up a frame.

> Inspect the frame for any pests or disease and have a good look at how much capped honey is on the frame. You'll know when your frames are full of honey because they will be heavy! Repeat with the remaining frames in the super.

> Check the brood chamber by removing the upper supers and the queen excluder and inspecting the bottom super.

> Very carefully remove the brood frames one by one, taking care not to injure or lose the queen in the process. You should be able to spot the queen among her thousands of workers because of her lengthened abdomen – sounds crazy, but once you know what to look for you can't miss her.

> If everything is looking ship-shape, gently reassemble the hive and inspect again in a couple of weeks.

HARVEST THE HONEY

Once your bees have filled a super with frames that are full of honey and capped with wax you can harvest your honey. Ideally, extraction from a Langstroth hive is performed with a honey extractor and a special heated blade. These will set you back a couple of hundred dollars but will last a lifetime.

> Set up your extractor well away from the hive so the bees aren't attracted to the harvested honey.

> Remove the honey-filled super from the hive and place the lid back on the lower supers. Lift the frames out of the super, shake off any bees and take it to your extracting station.

> Use the hot knife to remove the wax cappings from both sides of each frame and then place it in the extractor. Repeat until your extractor is full.

> Place a large clean bucket under the extractor outlet and spin the frames to remove the honey.

> Return the harvested frames to the super and repeat with the remaining frames.

> Once finished, return all the frames to the super and put the super back on top of the hive. The bees will soon refill the wax comb and you'll be ready for another harvest again in no time. Depending on how well the season is going and how vigorous your bees are, this could be as soon as 2 weeks! Just be sure that as summer ends, you always leave at least three frames full of honey in the hive so the bees have a food source over the cooler months, when pollen and nectar production in the surrounding plant life slows right down.

TIPS

> Plant bee-friendly flowering plants in your garden for your bees to forage. Try lavender, borage and sunflowers, or native plants like bottlebrush and tea tree.

> Be a calm beekeeper – slow, confident movements are less likely to startle bees; remember, a startled bee is more likely to sting you.

> If you do get stung, use your thumbnail or hive tool to scrape the stinger out. If you try to pinch it out, you'll actually squeeze more venom in.

> If you are stung and as a result start to swell around the throat and have trouble breathing, seek medical assistance immediately.

> Team up with another beekeeper who can mentor you.

> Register your hive. This is a legal requirement in all Australian states and territories, and is an essential biosecurity measure to protect European honey bees in Australia and the Australian honey industry from pest and disease outbreaks.

ROUGH GUIDE
TO PLANTING

Now that you've got your garden all ready to plant, it's time to get some seeds in the soil and start growing! To have success as a gardener you'll need to make sure you're planting veggies that are suitable for your climate and that you're planting them at the right time of year. I've taken some of the guesswork out by compiling this guide, which features the most popular fruit and vegetables. Use this to work out when to plant, how to care for all the different varieties, and how to know when your precious crops are ready to harvest. I understand you won't necessarily want to start growing everything at once, so I've also chucked in a bit of information about when each fruit or vegetable is in season and what to look for in the shops when you're buying them.

A quick reminder before you dive in – pretty much all fruit and vegetables grow best in rich free-draining soil that has been enriched with compost, worm castings or well-rotted manure, and the vast majority of plants will need at least 6 hours of sunlight a day to thrive. If you don't have the luxury of planting directly into the soil, remember that you can grow almost anything in a pot as long as the pot is big enough and is full of rich free-draining soil. Head back to the section on growing in pots if you need a refresher (see page 16).

Finally, I've divided the Australian continent into three rough climate zones: the tropics (which includes cities like Cairns and Darwin); warm climate (including Sydney, Brisbane and Perth); and cool climate (which would be places like Melbourne and Hobart). Of course Australia is a huge land mass and there will be loads of variation from one garden to the next. This is just a rough guide to get you started – no amount of advice from me can compare with the knowledge gained by growing in your own garden and learning by trial and error.

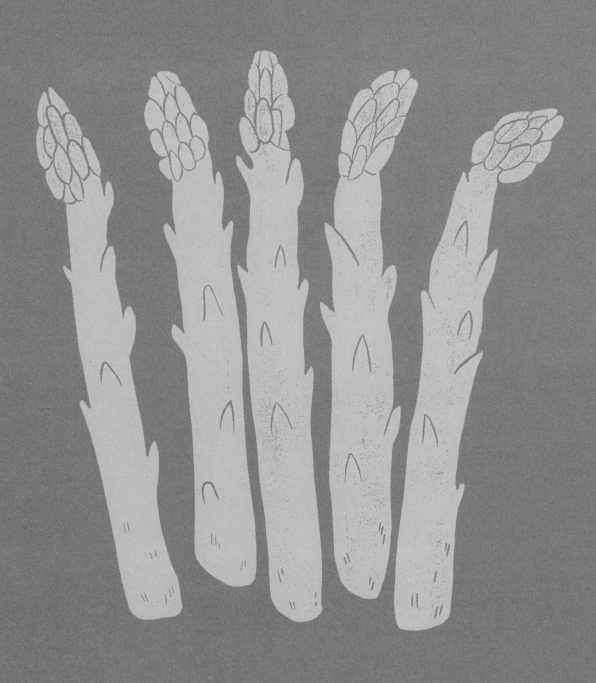

THESE CRISP SPEARS ARE THE EMBODIMENT OF SPRING FLAVOUR.

ASPARAGUS

My first experience with asparagus was eating the tinned stuff when I was a kid. Anyone who has tried tinned asparagus will understand why I didn't rate it very highly. However, when harvested straight from the garden or bought fresh and in season, asparagus is a true highlight on the culinary calendar. The emergence of those green tips in springtime is a welcome reminder that winter has come to an end and the warm days of summer are just around the corner. Asparagus is often harvested when there is little else coming out of the garden and, to me, these crisp spears, quickly cooked, are the embodiment of spring flavour.

GROWING

Position: Full sun

Seed or seedling: Both, though planting seedlings (crowns) is the most common method

Frost sensitive: The spears and foliage will tolerate light frosts

When to plant: In the cooler months when the crowns are dormant; this way they are well positioned to take advantage of the increasing warmth and day length in spring

> **Cool:** Jun–Sep
> **Warm:** May–Sep
> **Tropical:** Apr–Sep

BUYING

When: Spring

What to look for: Asparagus spears should be smooth and firm with tightly closed tips. A great test is to snap a spear towards the base – it should be crisp and juicy.

PLANTING AND MAINTENANCE

Dig a hole about 30 cm wide and 30 cm deep. If you plan on planting a few crowns, dig a trench the same width and depth and plant the crowns at 40 cm intervals. Make a small mound of dirt and place the asparagus crowns on top, making sure the roots are evenly spread and pointing down at roughly a 45-degree angle. Cover the crowns with a mixture of soil and compost, and water thoroughly. As the crowns start to grow, continue back-filling the trench until it's full.

Because it's a perennial plant, asparagus will require a little more TLC than a plant that is simply pulled out after harvest. When the fronds start to die off as winter approaches, cut off all the stems level with the soil and apply some mature compost or well-rotted manure, then a thick layer of mulch. This will ensure the plant has plenty of food for the next growing season and the soil is protected over winter. If you notice fewer spears coming up during spring, reduce your harvest, apply some compost and let the plant strengthen for the subsequent seasons.

HARVESTING

You'll have to exercise a bit of patience before you harvest your first crop of asparagus. As a general rule of thumb, you shouldn't harvest any spears in the first two years of growth and allow the plant to establish itself. When the third year finally rolls around, it's harvest time! Harvest spears that are thicker than a pencil and around 20 cm in length, with tightly closed tips. Use a sharp knife to cut the spears off just above the soil level. Leave any thin spears to continue growing throughout the season to enable the plant to store enough energy for the following season.

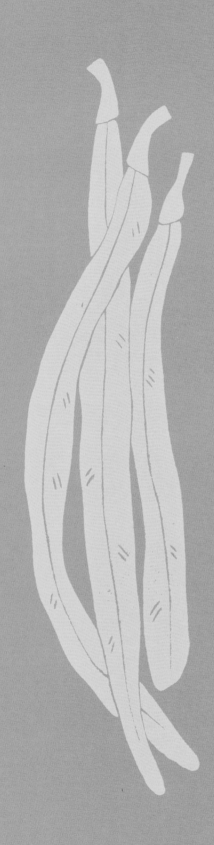

FRESHLY GROWN BEANS ARE CRISP, SWEET AND ABUNDANT.

BEANS

Green beans grown fresh in the garden are crisp, sweet and abundant, though funnily enough, not all varieties are green! The purple- and yellow-fruited varieties add both colour and height to the garden. Beans are a very versatile crop; some varieties provide a regular harvest throughout the growing season, while others can be dried and stored for use in the colder months. Climbing beans are also a great way to add height to your garden and to take advantage of vertical space.

GROWING

Position: Full sun

Seed or seedling: Seed

Frost sensitive: Yes

When to plant:

> **Cool:** Oct–Jan
> **Warm:** Sep–Feb
> **Tropical:** Apr–Jul

BUYING

When: Summer, autumn

What to look for: Beans should be well formed, brightly coloured and crisp enough to snap in half. Avoid beans that are floppy, browned or bruised.

PLANTING AND MAINTENANCE

Fork a little compost into the soil, then sow the beans directly into the soil spaced 15 cm apart. Wet the soil so that it is moist but not soggy and keep it that way until the seeds germinate (this should take about a week). Once the plants have emerged from the soil, surround them with mulch (as beans are shallow rooted and susceptible to drying out). They will require regular watering a couple of times a week and, although they are not heavy feeders, they'll still benefit from a feed with an organic liquid fertiliser every couple of weeks during the growing season. Climbing beans can reach up to 2 metres tall, so you'll need to provide trellising for them. I like to use pea and bean netting, but you can also use poles, bamboo or tree branches and some string.

HARVESTING

Beans will take 10–14 weeks to reach maturity. Harvest the pods when they are young and tender and, for best results, harvest every day or so.

EARTHY BEETROOT IS GREAT FOR ROASTING, PICKLING
AND INCLUDING IN SWEET BAKED TREATS.

BEETROOT

Sweet, earthy beetroot is easy to grow and is an incredibly nutritious, not to mention versatile, vegetable to include in your cooking. Beetroot can be grated and eaten raw, poached or roasted, is great for pickling and also lends itself to being sneakily included in sweet baked treats. The leaves are also perfect for adding to salads. Just be warned, beetroot will stain, so don't wear your finest white linens when you prepare it. If you're worried about purple-stained hands, grab some kitchen gloves.

GROWING

Position: Full sun

Seed or seedling: Both

Frost sensitive: No

When to plant: The sweetest beetroot is grown in the cooler months

> **Cool:** Sep–Feb
> **Warm:** Mar–Jul
> **Tropical:** Apr–Jun

BUYING

When: Spring, summer, autumn

What to look for: Look for beetroot with firm, split-free tubers. I also like to buy mine with the leaves and stems attached, both of which should be vibrant in colour and not limp. The stems are a great indication of freshness and can be used just like silverbeet in your cooking, while the leaves are great in salads.

PLANTING AND MAINTENANCE

Rake the beds smooth, then plant the beetroot seeds or seedlings into the soil with 10–15 cm spacings. Beetroot likes a consistent supply of water to prevent the tubers from drying out and cracking, so be sure to keep the soil moist with regular watering. They will also benefit from a fortnightly feed with an organic liquid fertiliser.

HARVESTING

Beetroot can be harvested at a variety of stages, depending on your preference. After 6 weeks you can take a few leaves here and there to add to a salad; make sure you harvest the leaves from the outside in and always leave at least five on the plant. After 8 weeks or so you can harvest the baby beets, which are perfect left whole, and after 12 weeks you can harvest the large beetroot. Don't let them grow any larger than a tennis ball or they will start to deteriorate in quality.

BROAD BEANS

Broad beans are a wonderful seasonal treat. They are the custodians of the winter garden, growing when all other plants have slowed to a standstill, then in spring, when the garden is looking sparse and a little sad, they produce an abundance of vibrant green pods. Some people may question the amount of work required to pod and remove the shell from the beans, but to them I say, PAH! There's something deeply meditative about preparing a bowl of broad beans and the sweet, fresh flavour more than justifies the effort.

GROWING

Position: Full sun, sheltered from the wind if possible

Seed or seedling: Seed

Frost sensitive: The flowers are but the foliage isn't, so don't expect fruit until after the worst of your frosts have passed

When to plant: Broad beans are a great crop to plant in your garden during winter – they fix nitrogen in the soil and will provide you with a tasty crop in spring when the rest of the garden is looking a little bare

> **Cool:** Mar–Aug
> **Warm:** Apr–Jun
> **Tropical:** Apr–July

BUYING

When: Spring

What to look for: Look for pods that are green, firm and crisp. The beans within the pod should be fully developed so you can feel them through the pod.

PLANTING AND MAINTENANCE

Plant broad beans with spacings of 20 cm. Broad beans are pretty low maintenance and will get by with only a little water and minimal feeding because they grow in the cooler months when there tends to be less soil evaporation and higher rainfall. In addition, they are a leguminous plant that fixes its own fertiliser from the atmosphere – how cool is that? If the plants are exposed to wind they can blow over so will benefit from some support. I like to place a stake on each corner of the growing bed and run some string around the border at various heights. It doesn't have to be anything particularly flash but a little bit of support will go a long way.

HARVESTING

Broad beans will grow throughout winter and start to produce beans in spring, with harvest taking place 15–20 weeks after planting. The pods can be harvested at a variety of stages: picked up to the thickness of your finger they can be eaten whole, but larger pods will need to be shelled. Pick regularly to encourage an abundant harvest.

BROCCOLI

Poor broccoli cops a bad rap, which is probably because many of us were forced to eat 'little trees' that had been boiled to within an inch of their soggy little lives when we were kids. Now we're all a bit older and wiser, it's clear that broccoli, when handled correctly, is actually delicious. It's also a great performer in the garden during the cooler months, with its slate-green foliage bringing a sense of abundance to the winter garden.

GROWING

Position: Full sun

Seed or seedling: Seedling

Frost sensitive: Will tolerate light frost

When to plant:

> **Cool:** All year
> **Warm:** Mar–Sep
> **Tropical:** Apr–Jul

BUYING

When: Spring, winter

What to look for: Look for bright green heads that have tight, compact clusters of florets. The stem should be strong and firm with no yellow leaves or florets.

PLANTING AND MAINTENANCE

Plant broccoli with spacings of 45 cm. Keep the soil around the broccoli plant well mulched and give it a feed with an organic liquid fertiliser every other week. Broccoli will benefit from a good watering a couple of times a week.

HARVESTING

Broccoli should be ready to harvest 8 weeks after planting. Harvest the main head when it appears fully formed (and before any flowers appear) by using a sharp knife to remove the head. After this first harvest, additional smaller flower shoots will grow and these should also be harvested before any flowers appear.

BRUSSELS SPROUTS

Brussels sprouts are a slow-growing plant that can be a bit of a challenge to get right for the home farmer. Seeds need to be sown when there's still plenty of warm weather left in the season to give the sprouts the best possible chance of reaching a decent size before the cold weather sets in. But when you do get them right they are a splendid sight in the garden and a very welcome addition to the kitchen table – just don't boil the life out of them! My advice is to undercook whole sprouts in boiling water, then split them in half and finish them in a frying pan with plenty of butter (or your preferred fat) and some strong flavours like bacon, anchovies or capers.

GROWING

Position: Full sun, sheltered from the wind

Seed or seedling: Seedling

Frost sensitive: No

When to plant:

> **Cool:** Oct–May
> **Warm:** Jan–Apr
> **Tropical:** Not suitable

BUYING

When: Autumn, winter

What to look for: Firm, tightly packed heads that are bright green and free from yellow leaves and black spots.

PLANTING AND MAINTENANCE

Plant brussels sprouts with spacings of 50 cm, then keep them well mulched and the soil consistently moist. Sprouts are heavy feeders so give them a feed of an organic liquid fertiliser every other week.

HARVESTING

Brussels sprouts are slow to grow and mature, taking upwards of 20 weeks to be ready for harvest. They mature from the base of the stem upwards and are ready to harvest when they are around 2.5 cm in diameter.

CABBAGE

Crisp and subtly sweet, cabbages are most welcome in my kitchen, in spite of their reputation for contributing to increased airflow after dinner! In the garden they appear abundant as their large leaves gently nurture the tightly packed heads that are forming in their eye. All the key varieties – red, green, savoy and Chinese – have similar growing requirements, so choose the one you like best.

GROWING

Position: Full sun

Seed or seedling: Seedling

Frost sensitive: No

When to plant:

> **Cool:** Aug–Mar
> **Warm:** All year
> **Tropical:** Apr–Aug

BUYING

When: Autumn, winter

What to look for: Look for firm, tightly packed heads that are brightly coloured and feel heavy for their size.

PLANTING AND MAINTENANCE

Plant cabbages with spacings of 60 cm. Cabbages will benefit from heavy mulching, watering a couple of times a week, and weekly feeds with an organic liquid fertiliser. If cabbage white butterflies (cabbage moths) are a problem in your area, use an insect mesh to cover the plants.

HARVESTING

Cabbages will mature between 11 and 15 weeks, and they are ready to harvest when the heads are firm. Use a sharp knife to cut the stem just below the head.

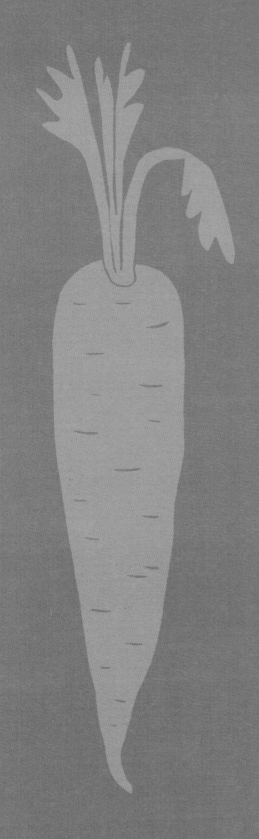

THE SWEETNESS OF A FRESHLY PULLED CARROT LEAVES
THE STORE-BOUGHT ONES FOR DEAD!

CARROTS

Having a dig around the garden, looking for a couple of choice carrots to pull up, is something that gives me a lot of pleasure. Maybe it's because all the action is happening under the ground and you never know just how magnificent a carrot will be until it erupts from the soil. You might ask yourself why it's worth the bother of growing carrots when you can buy them so cheaply, and if you're really pressed for space this is a valid point, but if you have the room, the sweetness of a freshly pulled carrot leaves the store-bought ones for dead!

GROWING

Position: Full sun

Seed or seedling: Seed

Frost sensitive: No

When to plant:

> **Cool:** Sep–Mar

> **Warm:** Aug–Apr

> **Tropical:** Mar–Oct

BUYING

When: All year

What to look for: Carrots should be crisp, firm and vibrant in colour. If they still have the tops attached, they should be bright green and look fresh, not wilted and limp.

PLANTING AND MAINTENANCE

Once the carrots have germinated, remove the weakest-looking seedlings so there is a 2–4 cm gap between those remaining. Repeat this process after a month, this time leaving an 8 cm gap between the remaining seedlings. Keep the carrot bed consistently moist and if having green tops on your carrots concerns you, mulch lightly over the top of the roots, leaving the leaves poking up through the mulch.

HARVESTING

Baby carrots will be good to go in 8 weeks or so and can usually be pulled up by hand, after gently loosening the soil around the top of the carrot. Larger carrots can take up to 16 weeks and will need to be lifted with a garden fork to avoid snapping the root when you pull them out.

CAULIFLOWER

Cauliflower is a fantastic vegetable to grow in your garden after your spring and summer crops start to fade away. You'll need to plant them when the weather is still warm, so they get a bit of a head start before the temperature drops right off, and if you get it right, you'll be rewarded with those amazing cumulus cloud–like heads. Cauliflowers can take up a fair bit of room so if you're pressed for space or growing in containers, look for miniature cultivars.

GROWING

Position: Full sun

Seed or seedling: Seed

Frost sensitive: Will tolerate light frost

When to plant:

> **Cool:** Nov–Jun
> **Warm:** Dec–Apr
> **Tropical:** Feb–May

BUYING

When: Spring, autumn, winter

What to look for: Heads should be a uniform white or cream and feel heavy for their size; they should also be tightly packed with no separated florets. If there are any leaves or stems attached, they should be crisp, green and fresh looking.

PLANTING AND MAINTENANCE

Plant seedlings 50 cm apart and mulch well around the plants. Water every couple of days throughout the growing season and apply a weekly feed with an organic liquid fertiliser once the heads start to form. To grow white sweet-tasting heads, you'll need to blanch them (not in the cooking sense) once they are about the size of a tennis ball. To do this, tie a couple of the cauliflower's leaves around the head so it's not exposed to direct sunlight. If cabbage white butterflies (cabbage moths) are giving you trouble, cover your plants with insect-excluding mesh.

HARVESTING

Cauliflowers take upwards of 12 weeks to mature and are ready when the head is full but the florets haven't started to separate.

CHILLIES

Chillies are the perfect addition to any home farmer's kitchen garden – they're relatively low maintenance, can be easily grown in pots and produce an abundance of fruit. I put them in the same boat as kitchen herbs when it comes to growing food. If you grow nothing else, grow chillies, as they are the ultimate way to add a bit of home-grown punch to your cooking.

GROWING

Position: Full sun, preferably in a spot sheltered from the wind

Seed or seedling: Both

Frost sensitive: Yes

When to plant:

> **Cool:** Sep–Nov
> **Warm:** Aug–Dec
> **Tropical:** Apr–Sep

BUYING

When: Summer, autumn

What to look for: Look for chillies with a vibrant colour and glossy taut skin.

PLANTING AND MAINTENANCE

Chillies benefit from rich soil, so fork through some compost or well-rotted manure before you get planting. Chillies can thrive in pots – just be sure to select a nice big one (I'd say at least 30 cm wide and 30 cm deep) and fill it with high-quality organic potting mix. Give your chillies a weekly feed with an organic liquid fertiliser, water every couple of days and keep the plant well mulched.

HARVESTING

Chillies take around 12 weeks to ripen, though they can be harvested at any time once they are full sized, no matter what colour they are.

THE FLAVOUR OF HOME-GROWN CORN WILL KNOCK YOUR SOCKS OFF!

CORN

Nothing makes a backyard veggie patch look more abundant than a stand of corn that's higher than your head and gently swaying in a summer breeze. But more importantly, the flavour of home-grown corn will knock your socks off, especially if you search out heirloom sweet corn seeds to grow.

GROWING

Position: Full sun

Seed or seedling: Seed

Frost sensitive: Yes

When to plant:

> **Cool:** Oct–Jan
> **Warm:** Sep–Feb
> **Tropical:** All year

BUYING

When: Summer, autumn

What to look for: The husk should be bright green and firmly wrapped. If the silks are still attached, they should be brown and not have turned black. Of course, you can also peel back a little of the husk to check that the kernels look firm and juicy.

PLANTING AND MAINTENANCE

Plant corn 20 cm apart and mulch around the seedlings to prevent weeds and conserve soil moisture. As an alternative to mulch, you could interplant the corn with a rambling vine like pumpkin or watermelon, which will grow around the corn stalks and protect the soil with its foliage. Corn is a fast-growing, hungry plant and will benefit from regular watering (every other day is fine) and weekly feeding with an organic liquid fertiliser.

HARVESTING

Corn will mature in around 10 weeks, with each plant producing a couple of cobs or more. The cobs are ready to harvest when the stringy bits at the top (known as silks) have turned brown. Double check by peeling back a little bit of husk – the kernels should look plump and juicy. Remove the cob easily from the plant by twisting it down sharply.

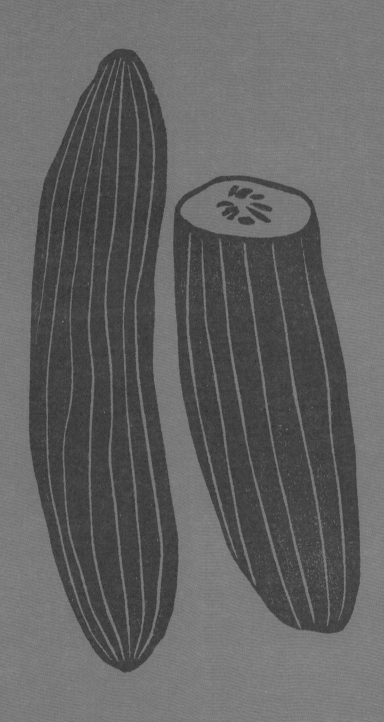

CUCUMBERS ARE CRUNCHY, FRESH AND PERFECT FOR A HOT SUMMER'S DAY.

CUCUMBERS

Cucumbers are one of my favourite summer veggies. They're so crunchy and fresh, and exactly what I feel like eating after a hot summer's day in the garden. The best thing is that they're both nourishing and hydrating. They can also be grown up a trellis or support pole, taking advantage of vertical space, making them a super-productive choice when you have limited room.

GROWING

Position: Full sun in cooler climates, though it benefits from a bit of shade in hot climates

Seed or seedling: Both

Frost sensitive: Yes

When to plant:

> **Cool:** Oct–Dec
> **Warm:** Sep–Jan
> **Tropical:** Jul–Oct

BUYING

When: Spring, summer, autumn

What to look for: Cucumbers should be crisp, firm and vibrantly coloured.

PLANTING AND MAINTENANCE

Plant cucumbers with spacings of 60 cm. They grow as a rambling vine and will benefit from being able to grow up a trellis, though if you have the space and don't mind going for a bit of a fossick when it's time to harvest, you can let them ramble across the ground, too. Cucumbers are hungry plants and will benefit from weekly feeds with an organic liquid fertiliser; they also like to have consistent moisture around their root zone, making them particularly well suited to a drip irrigation system (see page 34) laid under a deep mulch.

HARVESTING

Cucumbers will take around 8 weeks to reach maturity, though the fruit can be harvested at any size. You can let them grow large for slicing or harvest them young for eating whole or turning into pickles. Cucumbers are better harvested under-ripe than over, and should be cut from the vine with a sharp pair of scissors to prevent damage to the vine.

EGGPLANTS

Such a delicious vegetable! Eggplants are so versatile in the kitchen and pretty straightforward to grow in the garden. They are closely related to the tomato, so what's good for one is good for the other; if anything, eggplants like it even hotter!

GROWING

Position: Full sun

Seed or seedling: Seedling

Frost sensitive: Yes

When to plant:

> **Cool:** Sep–Nov
> **Warm:** Aug–Dec
> **Tropical:** Mar–Aug

BUYING

When: Summer, autumn

What to look for: Look for eggplants that have smooth, shiny skin, feel slightly firm to the touch and have a green stem.

PLANTING AND MAINTENANCE

Plant eggplants with spacings of 50 cm. They will benefit from watering a couple of times a week, along with a weekly feed with an organic liquid fertiliser. Eggplant plants can get very top heavy once their fruit starts to mature, so secure them to a tomato stake to prevent them from toppling over.

HARVESTING

It can take up to 12 weeks for eggplants to be ready for harvest. Knowing when to harvest them can be a bit of a balancing act – too early and there isn't much fruit for your efforts; too late and it will be full of seeds with thick skin, and will start to taste bitter. One of the best methods to find that sweet spot (other than good old trial and error) is to wait until the skin has a glossy shine to it.

KALE

I don't know who heads the marketing team for kale, but they definitely earn their keep. When I was a kid I'd never even heard of kale, but now it seems to have acquired superfood status! Whether you feel it deserves this or not, it definitely deserves a place in your garden; a well-tended kale plant will provide you with an abundance of nutritious leafy greens for months on end.

GROWING

Position: Full sun

Seed or seedling: Both

Frost sensitive: No

When to plant:

> **Cool:** All year
> **Warm:** Feb–Sep
> **Tropical:** Mar–Jul

BUYING

When: All year

What to look for: Leaves should be crisp, brightly coloured and mostly free from any holes caused by insect damage.

PLANTING AND MAINTENANCE

Space kale plants 30 cm apart. They are pretty low maintenance and you can get away with watering them once or twice a week and feeding them with an organic liquid fertiliser every other week. If they are being attacked by cabbage white butterflies (cabbage moths), protect them with an insect-excluding mesh.

HARVESTING

You can start harvesting kale leaves after about 8 weeks, picking the outer leaves first, and making sure you leave at least one-third of the leaves on the plant. If you do this, the plants will continue to grow and provide you with leaves for months.

LEEKS ARE PERFECT FOR DISHES WHERE ONIONS MIGHT BE OVERPOWERING.

LEEKS

Onion's sweeter and milder cousin, leeks are perfect for dishes where onions would be overpowering. They are a relatively simple crop to grow, unless you want to keep the stems nice and white, in which case they require a little more attention.

GROWING

Position: Full sun

Seed or seedling: Seedling

Frost sensitive: No

When to plant:

> **Cool:** Sep–Mar
> **Warm:** Aug–Apr
> **Tropical:** Mar–Jun

BUYING

When: All year

What to look for: Leeks should be crisp and firm with plenty of white or light green colour.

PLANTING AND MAINTENANCE

Dig a 15 cm deep trench, leaving the soil just to the side of it, and plant the leeks into the trench at 10–20 cm spacings. As the leeks grow, shovel a little more dirt into the trench and around the stems of the leeks. This process (called blanching) will maximise the amount of white stem your leeks have. If you can't be bothered or aren't fussed about green-stemmed leeks, just plant them into the ground as normal. Keep your leeks happy as they grow by watering them a couple of times a week and giving them a feed with an organic liquid fertiliser every other week.

HARVESTING

Leeks are ready to harvest after 20 weeks or so when the base of the stem is about 2.5 cm in diameter, but really, they can be harvested whenever they look big enough for your purposes. Thinner leeks can be pulled out of the ground by hand but larger ones will need to be lifted using a garden fork.

SWEET AND EARTHY WHEN COOKED, ONIONS ARE AN EVERYDAY STAPLE.

ONIONS

Astringent and eye-watering when raw, but sweet and earthy when cooked, onions are a staple ingredient in my cooking. Bought ones can be a little lacklustre but grown in your backyard they are like a completely different vegetable. Generally speaking, onions like to grow in the cooler months, though different varieties are more suited to some climates than others. Be sure to check on your seed packet or seedling tray that you have the right variety for your climate.

GROWING

Position: Full sun

Seed or seedling: Both

Frost sensitive: No

When to plant:

> **Cool:** Apr–Oct
> **Warm:** Mar–Sep
> **Tropical:** Not suitable

BUYING

When: All year

What to look for: Look for onions that have dry, delicate skin, feel heavy in the hand and are firm to the touch.

PLANTING AND MAINTENANCE

Onions don't like to grow in over-fertilised soils so plant them to follow heavy-feeding crops like corn or tomatoes. Sow seeds into a very shallow furrow that's only a couple of centimetres deep, then cover them back over with soil and water them in. Once germinated, thin out to spacings of 10 cm. Onions are pretty low maintenance and as long as they are watered a couple of times a week they shouldn't require a great deal of feeding. An application of an organic liquid fertiliser every couple of weeks will keep them nice and happy.

HARVESTING

Onions grow slowly and can be harvested and used at any stage you like really. For example, the sprouts from any thinning you might do make a great addition to salads. Fully developed bulbs will take at least 20 weeks, indicating they are ready when the green leaves at the top of the plant begin to turn brown. If you want to store your onions, pull them out of the ground, gently brush off any dirt and trim off any shrivelled leaves. Arrange them in a single layer somewhere dry, airy and out of direct sunlight and leave them to cure for 4 weeks or so. Once cured, place them somewhere cool and dark with good airflow. During the warm weather they'll keep for a couple of months, and will last up to 6 months in the cooler part of the year.

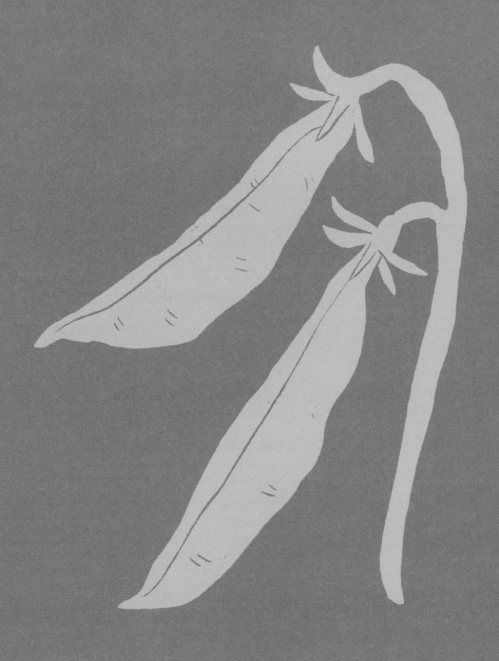

PEAS YIELD SWEET, CRISP DELICACIES THAT ARE BEST
ENJOYED STRAIGHT FROM THE VINE.

PEAS

Peas are a fantastic cool-season crop. They add welcome vertical texture to the winter garden and yield crisp, sweet delicacies that, really, are best enjoyed straight off the vine. If you have kids floating about, show them what mature peas taste like and then tell me you can't get them to eat veggies! Peas are also a great plant to grow if you're pressed for space – they will give you stacks of fruit for their relatively small footprint.

GROWING

Position: Full sun

Seed or seedling: Seed

Frost sensitive: No

When to plant:

> **Cool:** Jan–Oct
> **Warm:** Feb–Aug
> **Tropical:** Mar–Jul

BUYING

When: Spring, summer, autumn

What to look for: Pods should be intact and an evenly coloured bright green. The peas should be firm and fully developed.

PLANTING AND MAINTENANCE

To give your peas a head start, soak the seeds in water for 24 hours before planting. When planting, space the peas 15 cm apart. Peas can climb up to 2 metres tall so you will need some sort of trellis or pole structure for them. Peas hate being overwatered and should only be watered when the soil appears to have dried out, and even then, only around the base of the plant, taking care not to wet the foliage.

HARVESTING

Peas take 9–15 weeks to reach maturity, and will produce pods for around 3 weeks. Make sure you pick them regularly to encourage an abundant crop.

POTATOES

Who doesn't love a spud? They're so versatile in the kitchen, not to mention delicious. In the garden they are a relatively easy crop to grow and can be cultivated in a number of ways. They need fertile, free-draining and friable soil, and you can grow them in bags, pots, raised beds, wire cages or trenches. Just avoid growing them in a stack of old tyres because of the risk of heavy-metal contamination.

GROWING

Position: Full sun

Seed or seedling: Grown from 'seed' potatoes, which are available from good seed and garden suppliers

Frost sensitive: No

When to plant:

> **Cool:** Aug–Dec
> **Warm:** Jul–Dec
> **Tropical:** Apr–May

BUYING

When: All year, though new or baby potatoes start appearing around late spring/early summer.

What to look for: Look for spuds that have smooth skin and are firm to the touch. Avoid spongy or wrinkled potatoes, as well as those with any green patches.

PLANTING AND MAINTENANCE

Space plants 40 cm apart and plant them 10 cm into the ground. As the plant starts to grow green shoots, cover the shoots with soil to increase yield and to stop tubers from being exposed to sunlight and turning green. Potatoes don't like to be overwatered so make sure they are planted into well-draining soil and don't overwater them – a couple of times a week will be ample.

HARVESTING

Time to harvest can take between 10 and 20 weeks, depending on the variety and the desired size. New potatoes can be harvested as the first flowers start to appear, while the browning of the green foliage indicates that fully mature potatoes are ready to harvest.

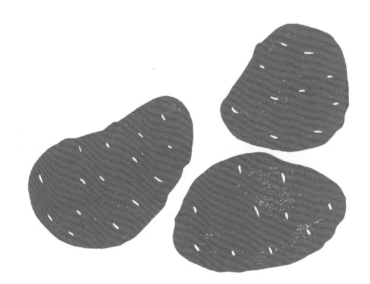

PUMPKIN

When conditions are right in your garden, pumpkins will grow like monsters! One minute you'll be tending a tiny seedling and the next thing you know it'll be wrapping a tendril around your leg and trying to pull you into the depths of the patch. Pumpkins tend to take up a lot of space but you can still grow them in smaller spaces by choosing bush varieties or training smaller fruiting varieties up a trellis.

GROWING

Position: Full sun

Seed or seedling: Both

Frost sensitive: Yes

When to plant:

> **Cool:** Oct–Dec
> **Warm:** Sep–Jan
> **Tropical:** All year

BUYING

When: Autumn, winter

What to look for: Look for pumpkins that feel firm and heavy for their size and have no soft spots.

PLANTING AND MAINTENANCE

Plant pumpkins with spacings of 1 metre. They are a voracious plant and will greatly benefit from watering every couple of days and a weekly feed with an organic liquid fertiliser.

HARVESTING

Pumpkins take up to 20 weeks to reach maturity, depending on the variety. You can tell when a pumpkin is ready because the skin will be thick, the tendrils nearest the pumpkin will be dead, and the pumpkin will sound hollow when tapped.

LOOK AFTER RHUBARB PROPERLY AND IT WILL PROVIDE YOU
WITH FLAVOURSOME STALKS FOR MANY YEARS.

RHUBARB

This is a great vegetable to grow as you will always have something to whip up into a dessert. Rhubarb is a perennial plant, and if you look after it properly it will continue to grow and provide you with flavoursome stalks for many years. A word of warning though: the leaves are very high in oxalic acid and, while you'd have to eat a bucket-load of them to be poisoned, you should always remove them before cooking.

GROWING

Position: Full sun, though it will benefit from afternoon shade during summer in warmer climates

Seed or seedling: Can be grown from seed or by dividing the roots of mature plants in late winter or early spring

Frost sensitive: No

When to plant:

> **Cool:** Oct–Nov
> **Warm:** Sep–Oct
> **Tropical:** Not suitable

BUYING

When: Spring, summer

What to look for: The stalks should be firm, crisp and blemish free. If the leaves are attached, they should look fresh and green.

PLANTING AND MAINTENANCE

Plant rhubarb crowns into fertile, well-drained soil spaced 1 metre apart. Mulch heavily around the plants and make sure they get weekly soakings and fortnightly feeds with an organic liquid fertiliser during summer. If any plants send up a flower spike, cut it out at the base, otherwise the plant will put all its efforts into growing seeds instead of tasty stalks. After 5 years the crowns can be divided and replanted elsewhere.

HARVESTING

Don't harvest during the first year so the plant can establish itself. After that, harvest the outer stalks as required. Remove them from the plant by pulling the stalks downward and to the side. Be sure to leave at least four stalks on the plant after harvesting.

SILVERBEET

Many people think of it as spinach but, while it may be a relative, silverbeet is actually more closely related to beetroot. Family connections aside, silverbeet is a must in everyone's garden – it's hardy and provides a continued harvest over a very long period. It's also an excellent plant to grow if you're new to gardening as it will be very forgiving of the stumbles of a novice.

GROWING

Position: Full sun, though it will benefit from afternoon shade during summer in warmer climates

Seed or seedling: Both

Frost sensitive: No

When to plant:

> **Cool:** Aug–Feb
> **Warm:** Jul–Mar
> **Tropical:** Apr–Jul

BUYING

When: Autumn, winter

What to look for: The leaves should look fresh and be dark green and glossy, while the stems should be firm and crisp.

PLANTING AND MAINTENANCE

Plant silverbeet with 25 cm spacings. The plant is very hardy and will only require watering once or twice a week and feeding with an organic liquid fertiliser every other week, if at all! As long as they are given a little extra water and some shade over the hot months of summer, silverbeet can live for up to 2 years.

HARVESTING

The first leaves are ready to harvest in around 8 weeks. Harvest the outside leaves first, always leaving at least one-third of the plant intact. Continual harvesting in this manner will encourage the plant to grow plenty of new leaves.

STRAWBERRIES

It's hard to beat ripe strawberries freshly harvested from your own garden. Their rich, sweet flavour bears almost no resemblance to the strawberries you buy in the supermarket. Strawberries will flourish in the ground or in pots, so they make an excellent addition for anyone with a small container garden. For best results, plant runners from your local nursery or a strawberry-growing friend who has healthy plants.

GROWING

Position: Full sun, though they will welcome a little afternoon shade in places with hot summers

Seed or seedling: Seedlings or by planting runners from established plants

Frost sensitive: The fruits are frost sensitive but the plant itself is not

When to plant:

> **Cool:** Sep–Nov
> **Warm:** Apr–Jul
> **Tropical:** Apr–May

BUYING

When: Fruit from southern states, mid spring–summer; fruit from northern states, late autumn–early spring

What to look for: Look for fruit that is bright red with no white around the stem. It should be firm, but not hard.

PLANTING AND MAINTENANCE

Plant strawberry crowns 30 cm apart at soil level. The plants will benefit from being surrounded by a heavy mulch to supress competition from weeds, retain soil moisture and protect the fruit from coming into contact with the soil. If runners appear, they can be pruned off and planted separately to become new plants. Water a couple of times a week during the growing season and apply a feed of an organic liquid fertiliser every fortnight to ensure juicy, flavoursome fruit. Ripe strawberries are also super attractive to all manner of devious, berry-hungry creatures, so it's worth protecting your crop with a bit of mesh when they are close to ripening.

HARVESTING

Strawberries will ripen around 4 weeks after the first flowers appear. Pick the fruit when they are fully and richly coloured.

SWEET POTATOES

Sweet potatoes grow as a vine that produces delicious underground tubers. They thrive in subtropical and tropical conditions, and when they're happy they can run rampant. They are extremely frost sensitive and will struggle to grow in cold climates, though I have heard of people having success by planting them in a warm, sheltered microclimate. Grown in the right climate, sweet potatoes are super hardy and are an easy way to grow bucket-loads of nutrient-dense food with minimal effort.

GROWING

Position: Full sun, though they will tolerate a bit of shade

Seed or seedling: Planted using a small piece of sweet potato that has sprouted (known as a slip)

Frost sensitive: Yes

When to plant:

> **Cool:** Not suitable
> **Warm:** Sep–Nov
> **Tropical:** All year

BUYING

When: Summer, autumn

What to look for: Sweet potatoes should be smooth, firm and free from sprouts, with undamaged skin.

PLANTING AND MAINTENANCE

Sweet potatoes can be grown by planting small tubers that have sprouted, or by producing slips. To make a slip, cut a runner from a healthy sweet potato vine to a length of around 15 cm and remove all the leaves except the ones at the tip. Plant the slips into the ground about 30 cm apart, with 1 metre between rows, leaving only the leaves above the ground. Keep sweet potatoes happy by watering them every couple of days and giving them a big feed with an organic liquid fertiliser every month.

HARVESTING

Tubers take around 4 months to mature; the vine will start to turn yellow when they are ready to harvest. Clear away the vine to reveal the base of the plant, then use a garden fork to start gently lifting the soil around 30 cm away from the base, so that you don't damage the tubers.

If you eat your sweet potatoes straight from the garden, you may be unpleasantly surprised to find they aren't that sweet. For the best flavour, sweet potatoes need to be 'cured', a process that converts the abundant starches in the tuber into natural sugars. To cure your freshly harvested sweet spuds, leave them to dry in a warm, sunny spot for an afternoon. Once the sun goes down, pop the tubers into an open cardboard box or ventilated crate and place them somewhere warm and dry to cure for a couple of weeks. I like to leave mine inside my shed up against the wall that gets the most sunshine on the outside. Curing not only enhances the flavour, it also increases the length of time you can store your sweet potatoes.

TOMATOES

Ask any food gardener, whether they are a first timer or a seasoned pro, what their number one plant to grow is and chances are they'll say tomatoes. The old adage that home-grown produce tastes better rings especially true for tomatoes. Seriously, you haven't lived until you've feasted on warm, sun-ripened tomatoes straight off the vine in your own backyard.

GROWING

Position: Full sun

Seed or seedling: Seedling

Frost sensitive: Yes

When to plant:

> **Cool:** Oct–Dec
> **Warm:** Aug–Jan
> **Tropical:** Mar–Jul
>   (can be grown during the
>   wet season but there is
>   an increased risk of disease)

BUYING

When: Summer, autumn

What to look for: Tomatoes should be plump, smooth and deeply coloured. Good tomatoes will also be wonderfully aromatic with that distinctive sharp, herbal smell.

PLANTING AND MAINTENANCE

Plant tomato seedlings into the soil right up to their lowest leaves, spacing them 50 cm apart. Tomatoes have a natural trailing habit and can be left to ramble all over the ground if you like – just be sure to mulch well around the plant so that as it grows and sets fruit, the fruit doesn't come into contact with the soil, which can cause it to rot. Alternatively, all tomatoes can be staked by driving a long hardwood stake into the ground next to the plant. As the plant grows, secure it loosely to the stake with cloth ties (I keep any worn-out t-shirts and cut them into strips to tie mine up). Tomatoes like to be watered every other day, and you should also give them a weekly feed with an organic liquid fertiliser.

HARVESTING

Tomatoes will mature in 7–13 weeks. If you're going to eat them straight off the vine wait until they are perfectly ripe; if you'd like to store them for a bit, harvest them when they are still a little firm.

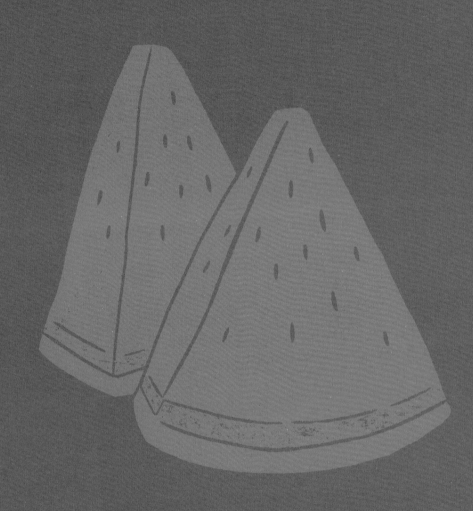

JUICY WATERMELON IS ONE OF THE REAL TREATS OF SUMMER.

WATERMELON

Eating a piece of sweet, juicy watermelon is one of the real treats of the summer growing season, and they don't taste any better than when you've grown them yourself. You may be surprised (shock horror!) to learn that home-grown watermelons contain seeds, though dealing with these little black bullets is a small price to pay for the amazing flavour.

GROWING

Position: Full sun

Seed or seedling: Both

Frost sensitive: Yes

When to plant:

> **Cool:** Oct–Dec
> **Warm:** Sep–Jan
> **Tropical:** Apr–Jul

BUYING

When: Summer, autumn

What to look for: Watermelons should feel heavy for their size, have a yellow patch on them where they were sitting on the ground, and sound hollow when tapped.

PLANTING AND MAINTENANCE

Plant watermelon seeds or seedlings with 1 metre spacings. During the growing season, water the vines a couple of times a week but not too much, as overwatering can result in bland or split fruit. For healthy plants and tasty fruit, feed the vine with an organic liquid fertiliser every week.

HARVESTING

Watermelons can take 12–20 weeks to ripen. When the fruit is ready to harvest, the tendrils and leaves of the fruiting stem will start dying off, there will be yellowing on the underside of the fruit, and the melon will make a hollow sound when tapped.

ZUCCHINI PLANTS ARE INCREDIBLY ABUNDANT,
PRODUCING A NEVER-ENDING STREAM OF FRUIT.

ZUCCHINI

Zucchini plants are incredibly abundant, producing what seems to be a never-ending stream of fruit. If you're a novice gardener, growing zucchini is a great way to get a bountiful harvest from a very forgiving plant. Just be careful not to get carried away and plant too many of them – the risk of drowning in a zucchini glut is very real!

GROWING

Position: Full sun

Seed or seedling: Both

Frost sensitive: Yes

When to plant:

> **Cool:** Oct–Dec
> **Warm:** Sep–Dec
> **Tropical:** All year

BUYING

When: Spring, summer, autumn

What to look for: Look for small to medium-sized zucchini that are firm, shiny and smooth. They should also be brightly and evenly coloured. It's rare to see really big zucchini on the shelf, but if you do it's best to split them in half, hollow out the seeds and roast them with a tasty filling.

PLANTING AND MAINTENANCE

Plant zucchini with 70 cm spacings and mulch well around them. Zucchini will thrive if you water them a couple of times a week – just be sure to water around the base of the plants rather than all over the leaves for maximum efficiency. To help the plant produce loads of zucchini, feed weekly with an organic liquid fertiliser.

HARVESTING

Zucchini plants will produce a stack of fruit anywhere from 6 weeks onwards. Check them regularly and harvest the fruit when they are still small to medium-sized – this will encourage the plant to produce more fruit.

We live in strange times. There's a proliferation of cooking programs on television, people's social media feeds are flooded with images of visually spectacular food, and every second person identifies as a 'foodie', yet, ironically, fewer people are actually cooking for themselves. It's almost like cooking has become a competitive sport rather than an act of love to nourish ourselves and those we care about.

Well my friends, I say it's time for us to reclaim our kitchens.

You might be thinking this is all very well for me because I used to be a chef so I know how it's done. But let me tell you, this has not always been the case. I vividly remember the first meal I tried to cook after moving out of home as a wide-eyed 18-year-old. I was living in a share house and cooking duties on that fateful night had fallen to me. I scanned our miserly pantry and fossicked among the cans of beer in the fridge, then assembled my stash of ingredients:

rice, soy sauce, ham and frozen peas. Too easy, I thought. Fried rice! How hard can it be? I chucked a pan on the stove, added a splash of oil and went in with the raw rice. I cooked it and cooked it and cooked it, but rather than softening, it just seemed to take on the texture of shiny gravel. (Yes, thank you, I am now very well aware that fried rice is made with rice that has already been cooked.) My housemates were pretty unimpressed with my crunchy, unpalatable disaster, and it was a long time before it was my turn to cook again. I'm sharing this story to reassure people that anyone can become a great cook, no matter what base you're starting from. It just takes a bit of practice.

Cue the recipe part of this book.

I've divided this section into two categories: vegetables/fruit and meat. The vegetable and fruit recipes far outnumber the meat ones because we need to be eating more plants, and as a home farmer you're far more likely to be producing vegetables than raising beef. The recipes in this section are arranged as an A–Z of commonly grown backyard veggies, with a recipe or two for each to get you inspired. This should make it easy for you to find a suitable recipe when you triumphantly harvest something special or a particular ingredient is at the height of its season. No meat features in the vegetable recipes so they are entirely vegetarian, and most of them can be modified to vegan with a few tweaks. I've kept the recipes as simple as possible and tried to feature only ingredients that are readily available at the average supermarket. I mean, I'd love it if everyone was growing all their own food but I'm a realist and know that, for some people, the supermarket is the only place to buy food.

The meat section focuses on secondary cuts and offal. The reasoning behind this is to address the perception that ethically raised meat has to be expensive. Secondary cuts and offal are more affordable, and are a great way for everyone to support our hardworking farmers. I put particular emphasis on beef and lamb because in southern Australia, the vast majority of this meat will have been raised on grass. If you decide to cook any of the pork or chicken recipes, I implore you to view them as a special treat and to purchase meat from an animal that has lived a life outdoors. Yes it may be more expensive, but please consider the ethical, environmental and social costs of factory-produced pork and chicken.

I'm really hoping you will use these recipes as a guide, rather than taking them as gospel. Feel free to tweak, substitute and experiment to your heart's content, and absolutely make them your own. Cooking should be a pleasure, so put on some of your favourite tunes, pour yourself a glass of something nice and get in that kitchen!

Granita

~~Pork Hock~~

~~Pea Fritters~~

Semi Freddo

~~Pork Belly~~

~~Grilled Zucchini~~

Dill Pickle.

Beetroot Brownies

Pumpkin Hash

Pot drizzle

· Chicken & Garden greens
Leeks

VEGETABLES & FRUIT.

ASPARAGUS: Baked asparagus with fried eggs and chilli breadcrumbs; Crispy crumbed asparagus with herby mayonnaise **BEANS:** Green bean and lentil salad with dried figs, feta and herbs **BEETROOT:** Beetroot and dark chocolate brownies **BROAD BEANS:** Broad bean falafel with pickled red onion and yoghurt–cucumber sauce; Broad beans, goat's curd and mustard greens **BROCCOLINI:** Sweet and sour broccolini and cannellini bean salad **BRUSSELS SPROUTS:** Shaved brussels sprout, apple and walnut salad; Pan-fried brussels sprouts with anchovy butter **CABBAGE:** Easy sauerkraut; Stuffed cabbage leaves in tomato sauce **CARROTS:** Crispy carrot and spring onion fritters; Carrot, almond and olive oil cake **CAULIFLOWER:** Roasted cauliflower with turmeric, chilli and lemon; Cheesy cauliflower and pasta bake **CHILLIES:** Fermented hot chilli sauce; Pickled green chillies **CORN:** Corn and black bean nachos with avocado yoghurt **CUCUMBERS:** Pickled dill cucumbers **EGGPLANTS:** Hearty slow-cooked eggplant curry **KALE:** Kale, herb and ricotta pie **LEEKS:** Charred leeks with yoghurt and capers **ONIONS:** Caramelised onion and lentil soup **PEAS:** Pea and feta fritters with labneh; Pea, barley and haloumi salad **POTATOES:** Potato and lemon drizzle cake **PUMPKIN:** Butternut pumpkin hash with fried eggs **RHUBARB:** Rhubarb and coconut crumble; Rhubarb, lemon and honey fool **SILVERBEET:** Silverbeet with spiced chickpeas and almonds **STRAWBERRIES:** Strawberry and vanilla semifreddo **SWEET POTATOES:** Creamy sweet potato and lentil bake **TOMATOES:** Really good homemade tomato sauce; Tomato, burrata and basil salad **WATERMELON:** Chargrilled watermelon with chilli, lime and mint; Watermelon granita **ZUCCHINI:** Zucchini and chocolate cake; Grilled zucchini with goat's cheese, herbs and hazelnuts

BAKED ASPARAGUS WITH FRIED EGGS AND CHILLI BREADCRUMBS

Asparagus is truly a seasonal treat, and its arrival in the garden heralds the beginning of another exciting growing season. Served here with crispy fried eggs and crunchy crumbs made from leftover bread, this is a fantastic dish to enjoy for breakfast bathed in the spring sunshine.

500 g asparagus spears, woody ends snapped off

olive oil, for cooking

salt and black pepper

1 large slice of stale sourdough, torn into pieces

2 dried red chillies

4 eggs

Preheat the oven to 250°C and line a baking tray with baking paper.

Toss the asparagus spears in a little olive oil, season with salt and pepper and place them on the prepared tray. Pop the tray in the oven and roast for about 15 minutes or until tender. Turn the oven off and leave the door open to keep the asparagus warm.

Meanwhile, put the stale bread in the bowl of a food processor, along with the chillies, a little olive oil and a good pinch of salt, and pulse to form coarse breadcrumbs.

Add a little olive oil to a large frying pan and fry the breadcrumbs over medium heat until golden and crispy. Set aside.

Wipe the frying pan clean, return to a medium–high heat and add a generous splash of olive oil. Crack the eggs into the pan. The oil should be hot enough so the eggs bubble and spit. Carefully spoon oil from the pan over the eggs to cook the tops. Once the eggs are crispy on the bottom with no runny bits on top, remove them from the pan.

Divide the asparagus among four plates, top each serve with a fried egg and scatter over the breadcrumbs.

SERVES 4

CRISPY CRUMBED ASPARAGUS
WITH HERBY MAYONNAISE

This one's a real favourite for me. The asparagus is buttery
and tender on the inside with a satisfying crunch on the outside.
The herby mayonnaise is a great way to use some fresh herbs
from your garden – I prefer a bit of everything but if you only
have one type of herb, that's fine too!

light olive oil, ghee or tallow,
for deep-frying

75 g (½ cup) plain flour

salt

2 eggs

60 g (1 cup) panko breadcrumbs

100 g (1 cup) finely
grated parmesan

1 bunch of asparagus spears,
woody ends snapped off

brassica flowers or other edible
flowers, to serve (optional)

HERBY MAYONNAISE

1 egg yolk

1 teaspoon dijon mustard

1 tablespoon white wine vinegar

pinch of salt

100 ml light olive oil

2 tablespoons finely chopped
flat-leaf parsley leaves

2 tablespoons finely chopped dill

2 tablepoons finely chopped chives

To make the mayo, combine the egg yolk, mustard, vinegar and salt
in a mixing bowl. Pour a steady trickle of olive oil into the bowl while
mixing constantly with a whisk. Once all the oil has been added and
the mayo has thickened, check the seasoning and adjust if necessary,
then fold in the herbs. Set aside.

Fill a large saucepan with your preferred deep-frying fat to a depth of
at least 5 cm, then heat over high heat to 180°C. If you don't have a
thermometer, place the handle of a wooden spoon in the oil – it should
bubble constantly but not vigorously.

To prepare your crumbing station you'll need three shallow bowls.
Tip the flour into the first bowl and season it with a pinch of salt;
crack the eggs into the second and lightly beat them; and combine the
breadcrumbs and parmesan in the third bowl. Roll the asparagus spears
in the flour, then dip them in the egg (shaking off any excess) and
finally roll them in the parmesan breadcrumbs.

Add the spears to the hot oil in batches, making sure you don't
overcrowd the pan, and cook for 1–2 minutes or until the breadcrumbs
are nicely golden. Remove the spears with tongs and drain them on
paper towel until just cool enough to handle.

Spread the herby mayo on a serving plate, arrange the asparagus on
top and scatter over some edible flowers, if you like.

SERVES 2 AS A STARTER

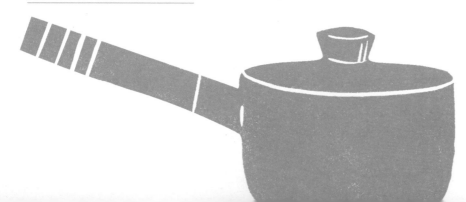

GREEN BEAN AND LENTIL SALAD
WITH DRIED FIGS, FETA AND HERBS

Green beans are so abundant in summer, but sadly they're often relegated to a mere side dish. Combined here with earthy lentils, salty feta and intensely sweet dried figs, this salad makes a great light lunch to enjoy outside at a nice shady table.

salt

400 g green beans, topped and tailed

400 g can brown lentils, drained and rinsed

12 dried figs, finely sliced

2 tablespoons olive oil

juice of 1 lemon

black pepper

200 g feta

½ bunch of flat-leaf parsley, leaves picked and roughly chopped

½ bunch of mint, leaves picked and roughly chopped

Fill a large saucepan with water and bring it to a rapid boil over high heat. Season the water generously with salt, enough to make it as salty as the sea.

Add the beans to the boiling water and cook for just 2 minutes – you want them to still have a bit of crunch. Remove the beans and plunge them into cold water to stop them cooking. Once the beans are cool, tip them into a colander and give them a good shake to remove any excess water.

In a large mixing bowl, combine the cooked beans and the lentils, fig, olive oil and lemon juice. Season with a little salt and pepper and give everything a good toss, then transfer the lot to a serving bowl.

Crumble the feta over the top, scatter with the herbs and serve.

SERVES 4 AS A LIGHT LUNCH

BEETROOT AND DARK CHOCOLATE BROWNIES

Beetroot and chocolate are a match made in heaven – they are both earthy and subtly sweet, and these brownies are the perfect way to bring them together. Adding vegetables to brownies doesn't exactly make them healthy, but these are so delicious you can pretend they are and have another.

1 beetroot (250 g)

250 g dark chocolate, roughly chopped

200 g unsalted butter, roughly diced

200 g caster sugar

3 eggs

100 g (1 cup) almond meal

1 teaspoon baking powder

140 g (1 cup) hazelnuts, lightly toasted and skins removed, roughly chopped

Place the beetroot in a medium saucepan and pour in enough water to cover. Bring to the boil over high heat, then reduce the heat and simmer gently for 30–40 minutes or until tender. Remove the beetroot from the water and set aside until cool enough to handle, then rub off the skin with your fingers (if you don't like the idea of purple hands, use a pair of rubber gloves). Grate the peeled beetroot and set aside.

Preheat the oven to 160°C. Grease a 25 cm square cake tin and line with baking paper.

Combine the chocolate and butter in a stainless-steel bowl, then place over a saucepan of gently simmering water and let them gently melt together. Make sure the bottom of the bowl doesn't touch the water.

Meanwhile, pop the sugar and eggs in another bowl and give them a good whisk to combine.

Once melted, pour the chocolate mixture into the egg mixture and whisk. Fold in the beetroot, almond meal, baking powder and hazelnuts.

Pour the mixture into the prepared tin and bake for about 40 minutes or until a knife or skewer inserted in the centre comes out clean.

Remove the brownie from the tin, then transfer to a wire rack and let it cool slightly. Cut into 20 squares and serve.

MAKES 20

BROAD BEAN FALAFEL WITH PICKLED RED ONION AND YOGHURT–CUCUMBER SAUCE

A bit of a variant on the usual chickpea-based falafel, I much prefer these broad bean ones, with their vibrant colour and delicate sweetness. This delicious meal is so moreish that it repays the effort of podding all those broad beans tenfold!

155 g (1 cup) Pickled Red Onion (page 274)

2 large handfuls of green leaves

8 small pita breads

BROAD BEAN FALAFEL

salt

1 kg broad beans in the pod (about 350 g podded)

3 garlic cloves, peeled

½ bunch of mint, leaves picked

½ bunch of flat-leaf parsley, leaves picked

1 teaspoon ground cumin

grated zest and juice of 1 lemon

1 tablespoon plain flour, plus extra if needed

black pepper

sunflower oil, for deep frying

YOGHURT–CUCUMBER SAUCE

1 Lebanese cucumber, halved lengthways and seeds removed, finely diced

250 g (1 cup) natural Greek-style yoghurt

grated zest and juice of ½ lemon

½ bunch of mint, leaves picked and roughly chopped

½ teaspoon salt

To make the falafel, fill a large saucepan with water and bring it to a rolling boil over high heat. Season the water generously with salt, enough to make it as salty as the sea.

Fill a large bowl with ice and water. Remove the broad beans from their pods and pop them in the boiling water for 10 seconds or so, then use a slotted spoon to transfer them to the ice bath. Pinch the end off the tough outer skin and give the shell a squeeze from the opposite end so the bright green bean inside pops out.

Place the shelled broad beans in the bowl of a food processor. Add the garlic, herbs, cumin and lemon zest and juice, and pulse until the mixture starts to resemble breadcrumbs. Add the flour and a little salt and pepper and pulse briefly to combine. Take a tablespoon of the mixture and try to roll it into a ball – if it won't bind, add a little more flour and pulse again until it does. Roll tablespoons of the mixture into falafels, then place them on a tray and refrigerate for about 15 minutes.

Pour the deep-frying oil into a large saucepan to a depth of 10 cm and heat over high heat to 180°C. If you don't have a thermometer, place the handle of a wooden spoon in the oil – it should bubble constantly but not vigorously.

While the oil is heating up, make the yoghurt–cucumber sauce. Place all the ingredients in a mixing bowl and stir to combine, then transfer to a serving bowl.

Once the oil is hot, add the falafel in batches and cook for about 3 minutes or until golden and cooked through. Remove with a slotted spoon and drain on paper towel.

To serve, arrange the falafel, yoghurt–cucumber sauce, pickled onion, green leaves and pita on a big serving platter. Get everyone to load up the pita breads and dig in.

SERVES 4

BROAD BEANS, GOAT'S CURD AND MUSTARD GREENS

This simple salad is full of flavour and texture. The sweet broad beans marry beautifully with the creamy curd, while the peppery leaves and crunchy hazelnuts add a bit of excitement for the senses.

salt

1 kg broad beans in the pod (about 350 g podded)

½ bunch of mint, leaves picked

140 g (1 cup) hazelnuts, lightly toasted and skins removed, roughly chopped

2 large handfuls of mustard greens (or watercress, mizuna or rocket)

100 g goat's curd

black pepper

DRESSING

3 tablespoons olive oil

1 tablespoon white wine vinegar

1 teaspoon dijon mustard

Fill a large saucepan with water and bring it to the boil over high heat. Season the water generously with salt, to make it as salty as the sea.

Fill a large bowl with ice and water. Remove the broad beans from their pods and pop them in the boiling water for 1 minute, then use a slotted spoon to transfer them to the ice bath.

Working over a mixing bowl, pinch the end off the tough outer skin and give the shell a squeeze from the opposite end so the bright green bean inside pops out. Add the mint, hazelnuts and mustard greens to the bowl.

To make the dressing, whisk together all the ingredients in a small bowl.

Add enough dressing to the salad to ensure it's lightly dressed (leftovers can be stored in a jar in the fridge for up to 2 weeks). Transfer to a large serving bowl, roughly break the curd over the top, season with salt and pepper and serve.

SERVES 4

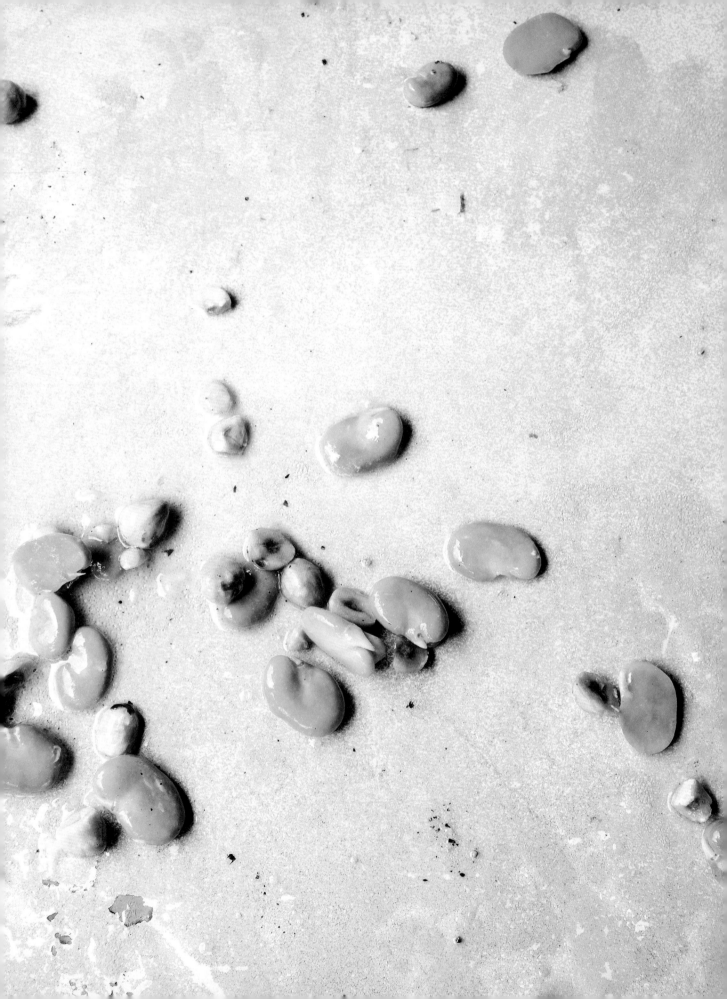

SWEET AND SOUR BROCCOLINI AND CANNELLINI BEAN SALAD

I use broccolini here as a broad term to describe any long-stemmed, loose-headed broccoli-like vegetable. That could be broccolini itself, sprouting broccoli or the shoots that grow on your broccoli plant after the main head has been harvested. I much prefer cooking with these than regular broccoli as I love the crunchiness of the lightly cooked stems and the delicate flavour of the florets.

salt

1 bunch of broccolini, ends trimmed

olive oil, for cooking

1 red onion, finely sliced

4 garlic cloves, finely chopped

100 g raisins

400 g can cannellini beans, drained and rinsed

finely grated zest and juice of 1 lemon

½ bunch of flat-leaf parsley, leaves picked and roughly chopped

50 g parmesan

Fill a large saucepan with water and bring it to a rolling boil over high heat. Season the water generously with salt, enough to make it as salty as the sea. Add the broccolini and cook for about 2 minutes or until the stems are still slightly crunchy. Remove the broccolini and plunge it into cold water to stop it cooking.

Heat a splash of olive oil in a large frying pan over medium heat, add the onion and gently fry for 2 minutes. Stir in the garlic and cook for another 2 minutes or until softened.

Drain the broccolini and add it to the pan, along with the raisins, cannellini beans and lemon zest and juice. Give everything a good toss. Check and adjust the seasoning and add a little more olive oil if the mixture seems a bit dry.

Scatter over the parsley and give everything one last mix, then transfer the whole lot to a serving bowl. Finely grate the parmesan over the top and serve.

SERVES 4

SHAVED BRUSSELS SPROUT, APPLE AND WALNUT SALAD

Raw brussels sprouts. It sounds like every child's nightmare, but in this simple recipe the thinly shaved leaves form the basis of a fantastically crisp yet delicately sweet salad. I love it.

500 g brussels sprouts

1 apple, cored and cut into matchsticks

200 g (2 cups) walnuts, toasted and roughly chopped

100 g (1 cup) grated parmesan

DRESSING

3 tablespoons apple cider vinegar

3 tablespoons olive oil

2 teaspoons dijon mustard

Remove any loose and discoloured outer leaves from the sprouts then, holding the stem, run the sprouts over a mandoline (or slice as finely as possible with a sharp knife). Combine the shaved sprouts with the apple and walnuts.

To make the dressing, whisk together all the ingredients in a small bowl.

Pour the dressing over the salad and toss to coat evenly. Scatter the parmesan over, toss again, then transfer to a large bowl and serve.

SERVES 4 AS A SIDE

PAN-FRIED BRUSSELS SPROUTS
WITH ANCHOVY BUTTER

Poor brussels sprouts – they cop such a bad rap, but it's not their fault that Nan used to boil them up into a soggy mess. To allay any misgivings you may have about sprouts you need to add butter, and don't be shy about it. Here, the tightly wrapped leaves are lightly caramelised in the pan, becoming the perfect companions for the salty punch of the anchovy butter.

salt

500 g brussels sprouts

100 g butter, softened

2 anchovy fillets, finely chopped

2 tablespoons capers, rinsed

2 garlic cloves, finely chopped

olive oil, for cooking

1 bunch of flat-leaf parsley, leaves picked and roughly chopped

juice of 1 lemon

black pepper

Fill a large saucepan with water and bring it to a rolling boil over high heat. Season the water generously with salt, enough to make it as salty as the sea.

While the water is coming to the boil, remove any loose and discoloured outer leaves from the sprouts and use a paring knife to score a cross in the base of the stem. Drop the sprouts into the boiling water and cook for 3 minutes or until the tip of a knife can be inserted into the stem with minimal resistance. Drain the sprouts and cut them into halves or quarters, depending on their size.

Combine the butter, anchovy, capers and garlic in a bowl.

Heat a splash of olive oil in a large frying pan over high heat. Add the sprouts and cook until they are nicely browned. Pop the anchovy butter in the pan and cook until it foams and starts to smell nutty. Add the parsley and lemon juice and season with salt and pepper. Tip into a bowl and serve.

SERVES 4 AS A SIDE

EASY SAUERKRAUT

I used to think that I didn't like sauerkraut. I don't know why – I'd never even tried it – I just couldn't imagine how fermented cabbage could taste good. Eventually I made a batch and realised how silly I'd been; this stuff tastes sensational, and it's so easy to make. Now I eat sauerkraut with just about everything, for breakfast, lunch and dinner (though I'm still trying to figure out how to make it work for dessert). This recipe is a good starting point for your cabbage fermenting journey, but feel free to experiment with other spices and substitute the white cabbage for savoy, red cabbage, Chinese cabbage or a mixture of all four!

1 white cabbage (about 1 kg)

1½ tablespoons sea salt

1 teaspoon caraway seeds

1 teaspoon dill seeds

1 teaspoon juniper berries

Remove any discoloured or limp outer leaves from the cabbage, then cut it into quarters and remove the woody core. Using a mandoline, sharp knife or food processor (in my order of preference), shred the leaves as thinly as possible.

Transfer the cabbage to a large mixing bowl and sprinkle over the salt. Make sure your hands are very clean, then massage the salt into the cabbage – really concentrate on trying to break down the fibres. After 5–10 minutes the cabbage will start to soften and release water. Mix through the caraway seeds, dill seeds and juniper berries.

Transfer the cabbage to a 1-litre sterilised jar (see page 278), pressing down as you go to make sure there are no pockets of air (this job is a great deal easier if you have a wide-mouthed funnel). Pour the released liquid over the top, then find something like a cup or smaller jar and put it in the big jar to weigh down the cabbage. Don't worry if it isn't fully submerged at this stage.

Place your jar somewhere cool and out of direct sunlight and press the weight down every so often. If the cabbage isn't completely submerged after 24 hours, make a brine mixture using the ratio of 250 ml (1 cup) of water to 1 teaspoon of salt, and top up the jar until the cabbage is entirely covered in liquid.

Now it's time to let the microorganisms work their magic. It will take anywhere from 3 days to 6 weeks to finish your sauerkraut, depending on factors such as ambient temperature and personal preference. The best way to determine if it's ready is to have a small taste every other day – you want the 'kraut to be sour and still have some crunch.

When it has fermented to your liking, transfer the jar to the fridge and use as you please. It will keep for up to 6 months.

MAKES ABOUT 1 KG

STUFFED CABBAGE LEAVES IN TOMATO SAUCE

There is something immensely satisfying about spooning these tasty cabbage parcels out of a rich tomato sauce. That said, preparing the leaves and rolling the parcels can be a little fiddly (check out the next page for some helpful photos), so this is the kind of recipe I cook for a Sunday dinner, when I have the time to really relish the process.

210 g (1 cup) brown rice

olive oil, for cooking

500 ml (2 cups) water or stock of your choice

salt

1 savoy cabbage

1 onion, finely diced

4 garlic cloves, finely chopped

2 teaspoons ground cumin

1 carrot, finely diced

2 celery stalks, finely diced

150 g (1 cup) currants

400 g can brown lentils, drained and rinsed

½ bunch of flat-leaf parsley, leaves picked and roughly chopped

juice of 1 lemon

black pepper

750 ml (3 cups) passata

Give the rice a good rinse under cold running water and shake out any excess water.

Heat a splash of olive oil in a saucepan over medium heat, add the rice and cook, stirring, for a couple of minutes. Pour in the water or stock and bring to the boil, then reduce the heat to low. Cover and simmer gently for 45 minutes or until the rice is cooked, then remove from the heat and leave to stand for 10 minutes.

Fill a large saucepan with water and bring it to the boil over high heat. Season the water generously with salt, to make it as salty as the sea.

Use a sharp knife to separate the base of the cabbage leaves from the stem and remove 12 whole leaves. Add the leaves to the pan and blanch for 2 minutes, then remove and pat them dry between a couple of clean tea towels. Save the remaining cabbage for another recipe.

Preheat the oven to 180°C.

Heat a splash of olive oil in a large frying pan over medium heat. Pop the onion in the pan and cook for 2–3 minutes or until translucent, then add the garlic and cumin and cook for another couple of minutes. Stir in the carrot and celery and cook for 3 minutes, then add the cooked rice and the currants, lentils, parsley and lemon juice. Season with salt and pepper and mix well, then remove the pan from the heat.

Lay out a cabbage leaf on a clean surface and place a big spoonful (technically, one-twelfth) of the stuffing mixture in the centre. Fold in the sides, then roll up the leaf from the stem end. Repeat with the remaining leaves and filling. Arrange the stuffed leaves snugly in a single layer in a deep baking dish, then pour over the passata. Place the dish in the oven and bake for 30 minutes.

When you're ready to eat, use an egg flip to lift the stuffed leaves onto plates. Spoon over the tomato passata and serve.

SERVES 4

CRISPY CARROT AND SPRING ONION FRITTERS

These fritters are subtly sweet and a little smoky, and they make a great lunch or light dinner. Because the carrots are grated it's a terrific way to use up any that are a little gnarly – they'll still taste amazing.

4 carrots (about 500 g), peeled and grated

3 spring onions, green and white parts finely chopped

3 eggs, lightly beaten

1 teaspoon smoked paprika

2 tablespoons plain flour

salt and black pepper

olive oil, for cooking

1 handful of coriander leaves

250 g (1 cup) natural Greek-style yoghurt

2 handfuls of leafy greens (such as rocket or mizuna)

lemon wedges, to serve

Combine the carrot, spring onion, egg, paprika and flour in a mixing bowl and season with a little salt and pepper.

Heat a large frying pan over medium heat and add enough olive oil to coat the base of the pan. Take a heaped tablespoon of the carrot mixture and squeeze out any excess moisture, then pop it in the pan and use the back of the spoon to flatten it out to a thickness of about 1 cm. Repeat until your pan is full but not overcrowded (you will need to cook the fritters in a few batches).

Fry for around 3 minutes or until a golden crust has formed on the base, then flip the fritters over and fry for another 3 minutes or until golden and cooked through. Transfer to a plate and cover to keep warm while you cook the remaining fritters.

Divide the fritters among four plates, sprinkle with salt, garnish with the coriander and serve with the yoghurt, greens and lemon wedges.

SERVES 4

CARROT, ALMOND AND OLIVE OIL CAKE

If you put veggies in a cake it's technically a health food, right? Well maybe not, but the carrots definitely add an earthy sweetness to this moist, dense cake that makes it very hard to resist.

3 carrots (about 450 g), peeled and grated

180 g caster sugar

230 g almond meal

2 teaspoons baking powder

2 eggs, lightly beaten

100 ml olive oil

finely grated zest and juice of 1 lemon

100 g flaked almonds

icing sugar, for dusting

nasturtium flowers and leaves, to decorate (optional)

double cream, to serve

Preheat the oven to 160°C. Grease a 23 cm springform tin and line with baking paper.

Combine the carrot, sugar, almond meal and baking powder in a large mixing bowl. Add the egg, olive oil and lemon zest and juice, and use a wooden spoon to bring it all together.

Transfer the batter to the prepared tin and give it a tap on the bench to flatten it out. Sprinkle the flaked almonds evenly over the top.

Bake for 35 minutes or until a skewer inserted in the centre comes out clean. Check the cake after 20 minutes or so – if the flaked almonds are becoming too brown, cover the tin with foil for the remainder of the cooking time. Remove the cake from the oven and let it cool slightly in the tin.

When you're ready to eat, remove the cake from the tin and place on a serving plate. Lightly dust the top with icing sugar and decorate with nasturtiums, if you like. Serve with big dollops of double cream.

SERVES 8

ROASTED CAULIFLOWER WITH
TURMERIC, CHILLI AND LEMON

Cauliflower is perfect for roasting – all the little nooks and crannies in the florets become crisp and caramelised, and the flesh tender and creamy. Here, the chilli, turmeric and curry powder add a real kick to the cauliflower, making it perfect to serve with big flavours like barbecued meat.

1 large head of cauliflower, broken into bite-sized florets

1 teaspoon ground turmeric

1 teaspoon curry powder

olive oil, for drizzling

salt and black pepper

1 long red chilli, finely sliced

½ bunch of flat-leaf parsley, leaves picked and roughly torn

lemon wedges, to serve

Preheat the oven to 220°C and line a large baking tray with baking paper.

Place the cauliflower florets in a large mixing bowl, add the turmeric, curry powder and a generous drizzle of olive oil and give everything a good toss so the cauliflower is evenly coated.

Transfer the cauliflower to the prepared tray and spread it all out in a single layer. Season with a bit of salt and pepper, then pop the tray in the oven and roast for about 20 minutes or until the cauliflower is nicely brown and tender.

Remove the tray from the oven and transfer the florets to a serving platter. Sprinkle over the chilli and parsley and serve with lemon wedges for squeezing over.

SERVES 4 AS A SIDE

CHEESY CAULIFLOWER AND PASTA BAKE

The pairing of cauliflower and cheese is hard to beat, and this creamy bake never fails to get my tastebuds excited – there's just something so irresistible about all the brown crispy bits and thick sauce bubbling volcanically fresh out of the oven. It's also the perfect way to use any leftover cooked pasta you might have lurking in the fridge.

salt

1 head of cauliflower, broken into bite-sized florets

250 g cooked tubular pasta (such as macaroni, penne or elbows)

750 ml (3 cups) thickened cream

125 g (1 cup) grated cheddar

2 teaspoons mustard powder

black pepper

1 handful of thyme leaves

Preheat the oven to 200°C.

Fill a large saucepan with water and bring it to a rolling boil over high heat. Season the water generously with salt, enough to make it as salty as the sea. Add the cauliflower and cook for 4 minutes – no more as you still want it to be slightly firm. Drain well.

Place the cauliflower and pasta in a deep baking dish and toss together well.

Place the cream, cheese and mustard powder in a mixing bowl, season with salt and pepper and mix together well. Pour it evenly over the pasta and cauliflower.

Bake for about 20 minutes or until the top starts to brown and bubble. Scatter the thyme leaves over the top and serve.

SERVES 4

FERMENTED HOT CHILLI SAUCE

I'm a chilli fiend, and this sauce is the perfect way to preserve a bumper chilli crop so you always have a splash of summer heat in a bottle. It's hot, tangy and goes with just about anything. You might want to make a double batch!

1 kg long red chillies, stems removed and roughly chopped

6 garlic cloves, roughly chopped

2 tablespoons sea salt

BRINE SOLUTION

30 g sea salt

1 litre filtered water

To make the brine solution, combine the salt and water in a saucepan over high heat and bring to the boil, stirring until the salt has dissolved. Remove from the heat and let the brine cool to room temperature.

Combine the chilli and garlic in a bowl and stir in the salt. Transfer the chilli mixture to a large sterilised jar (see page 278) and pour over enough of the brine solution to cover it completely. (Reserve any remaining brine in the fridge for future fermenting projects.)

Take a small piece of clean cloth (such as muslin or a Chux cloth) and secure it over the top of the jar with a rubber band, then place the jar somewhere with a stable temperature that's out of direct sunlight. Leave the sauce to ferment for about 2 weeks, though I do like to check it and give the whole lot a stir every couple of days. If a white film forms on the top, it's not harmful so don't despair – just scoop it out and discard, then give the mixture a stir and put the cloth back on top.

At about the 2-week mark, taste the chilli mixture; if it is sour with that fermented 'tang' you're good to go. If not, leave it for another day or two and taste it again.

Strain the chilli mixture, reserving the brine solution to kickstart your next fermentation, if you like. Blend the chillies using a hand-held blender or food processor. Finish the sauce by pushing the blended chillies through a fine-mesh strainer using a wooden spoon. If it's a little thin for your liking, you can thicken it with a slurry made from 1 teaspoon of arrowroot powder and 2 teaspoons of water. Transfer the sauce to a medium saucepan and reduce it over low heat to your desired consistency.

Pour the sauce into sterilised jars and pop it in the fridge, where it will keep for a couple of months. Though in my house, it never lasts that long!

MAKES 500 ML (2 CUPS)

PICKLED GREEN CHILLIES

I first tried these pickled chillies at an Egyptian restaurant and was instantly hooked. They are everything I look for in a pickle: tangy, crisp and packed full of flavour. They make a wonderful addition to a plate of snacks, served alongside cured meats and cheeses or, if you're like me, enjoy them straight from the jar.

1 kg long thin green chillies, stems trimmed short

750 ml (3 cups) white wine vinegar

1 tablespoon black peppercorns

2 teaspoons sea salt

2 teaspoons caster sugar

Use the tip of a sharp knife to prick each chilli a couple of times; this will allow the pickling solution to penetrate the chillies. Stuff the chillies into two 500 ml sterilised jars with lids (see page 278), nice and tight.

Combine the vinegar, peppercorns, salt, sugar and 250 ml (1 cup) of water in a saucepan and bring to the boil, giving it the odd stir to make sure the salt and sugar dissolve.

Allow the pickling solution to cool ever so slightly (about 5 minutes), then pour it into the jars, ensuring the chillies are totally submerged and the liquid is about 1 cm below the rim of each jar. Give the rims a wipe with a clean cloth if required, then pop the lids on and screw them shut. At this point you can put the jars in the fridge and use them straight away. Like this they will keep for 1 month, or you can heat treat them and store them in the pantry.

To heat treat the jars, place a tea towel on the bottom of a saucepan that is deeper than the height of the jars and place the jars on top, making sure they are not touching each other or the side of the pan (this may cause them to crack during boiling).

Fill the saucepan with enough water to cover the jars, and bring to the boil. Boil for 10 minutes, then kill the heat and leave until the water is cool enough for you to safely remove the jars. Wipe them dry, then store them somewhere cool and dark for up to 2 years. Once opened, store the jars in the fridge for up to 1 month.

MAKES 2 × 500 ML JARS

CORN AND BLACK BEAN NACHOS WITH AVOCADO YOGHURT

This is one of those quick-to-assemble dishes I like to throw together in summer when the days are long and I want to spend more time outside than in the kitchen. The caramelised corn kernels are little bombs of flavour and the black beans make this a hearty meat-free meal that is best eaten with your fingers.

olive oil, for cooking

4 corn cobs, silks removed, kernels cut from the cob

2 teaspoons ground cumin

2 teaspoons dried oregano

2 teaspoons sweet paprika

400 g can black beans, drained and rinsed

400 g plain corn chips

200 g grated cheddar

AVOCADO YOGHURT

1 avocado

125 g (½ cup) natural Greek-style yoghurt

TO SERVE

1 bunch of coriander, leaves picked

1 red onion, finely diced

Fermented Hot Chilli Sauce (page 162) or your other favourite chilli sauce

2 limes, cut into wedges

Preheat the oven to 200°C.

Heat a large frying pan over medium–high heat and add a good splash of olive oil. Add the corn and cook for 5 minutes or until it starts to brown up nicely, then add the cumin, oregano and paprika and cook for 2 minutes. Stir in the beans and cook for a further 2 minutes. Remove the pan from the heat.

Arrange one-third of the corn chips over the base of a large baking tray, then top with one-third of the corn mixture and one-third of the cheese. Repeat these layers twice more, then bake for 20 minutes.

Meanwhile, to make the avocado yoghurt, place the avocado flesh and the yoghurt in the bowl of a food processor and blend until smooth.

Remove the nachos from the oven and let it cool for a few minutes. Spoon over the avocado yoghurt and top with the coriander, red onion and chilli sauce. Serve with lime wedges for squeezing over.

SERVES 4

PICKLED DILL CUCUMBERS

Salty, tangy and crunchy, these pickled cucumbers are the perfect way to preserve a glut of cucumbers. They keep for ages so I often make a double batch to ensure I have always have some on hand.

4 dill sprigs

1 kg baby cucumbers, freshly picked or purchased that day

400 ml white wine vinegar

2 teaspoons mustard seeds

30 g sea salt

You will need four 500 ml jars for this recipe. Place a tea towel on the bottom of a large saucepan that is deeper than the height of the jars. Fill the pan with water and bring it to the boil.

Meanwhile, place a dill sprig in each of the four jars, then tightly pack in the cucumbers, being sure to leave just over 1 cm of space at the top. Combine the vinegar, mustard seeds, salt and 400 ml of water in a saucepan and bring to the boil, giving it the odd stir to make sure the salt dissolves. Pour the hot pickling solution into the jars, ensuring the cucumbers are totally submerged and the liquid is about 1 cm below the rim of each jar.

Give the jars a gentle tap on the bench to remove any air bubbles. Wipe the rims with a clean cloth if required, then pop the lids on and screw them shut. Using tongs, carefully lower the jars into the boiling water so they are submerged, making sure that they are not touching each other or the side of the pan (this may cause them to crack during boiling). Boil for 10 minutes.

Grab the tongs again and carefully remove the jars from the water, then allow to cool on the bench for 24 hours. Once they've cooled you can eat them if you must, but waiting a month will give you much more delicious pickles!

Store in the pantry for up to 2 years. Once opened, store the jars in the fridge for up to a year – if they last that long.

MAKES 4 × 500 ML JARS

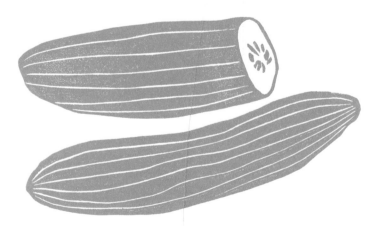

HEARTY SLOW-COOKED EGGPLANT CURRY

Eggplant is my favourite vegetable to add to a curry. When cooked slowly, it becomes incredibly meaty and creamy, resulting in a delicious and nourishing meal. Don't skimp on the yoghurt and coriander at the end – they really bring everything together.

olive oil, for cooking

2 large eggplants, cut into bite-sized chunks

2 onions, finely diced

8 garlic cloves, finely chopped

2 long red chillies, finely sliced

2 teaspoons ground coriander

2 teaspoons ground cumin

2 teaspoons ground turmeric

2 × 400 g cans chopped tomatoes

400 ml vegetable stock or water

cooked brown rice, to serve

natural Greek-style yoghurt, to serve

1 handful of coriander leaves

Heat a large deep frying pan over medium heat and add enough olive oil to lightly coat the base. Add the eggplant and onion and cook, stirring, for 5 minutes, then add the garlic, chilli and ground spices and cook for another 5 minutes.

Pour the tomatoes into the pan, add the stock or water and bring to a simmer, then reduce the heat to super low and cook gently for 30 minutes.

To serve, place a generous spoonful of rice in each bowl and spoon the curry over the top. Finish with a big dollop of yoghurt and a scattering of coriander leaves.

SERVES 4

KALE, HERB AND RICOTTA PIE

At various times of the year I have stacks of kale in the garden and this recipe is one of my favourite ways to put it to good use. It's quick to throw together and the kale and creamy ricotta team beautifully with the golden, flaky pastry.

olive oil, for cooking

1 onion, finely diced

2 large bunches of kale
(about 1 kg), stalks removed,
leaves shredded

400 g fresh ricotta, well drained

2 eggs, lightly beaten

½ bunch of dill, finely chopped

½ bunch of mint, leaves picked
and finely chopped

salt and black pepper

375 g packet of filo pastry, thawed

100 g butter, melted

Preheat the oven to 180°C.

Heat a large frying pan over medium heat and add a splash of olive oil. Add the onion and cook for 5 minutes, then toss in the kale and cook for a further 5 minutes. Transfer the whole lot to a large mixing bowl.

Add the ricotta, egg, dill and mint to the bowl and give it a good mix. Season with salt and pepper, then pop it to one side.

Lay out your filo sheets on the bench and cover with a clean damp tea towel to stop them drying out.

Brush a 30 cm pie dish with some of the melted butter. Arrange four sheets of filo in the dish so they are overlapping, with some of the pastry hanging over the edge. Brush with a little more butter and add another four overlapping sheets of pastry, then brush with butter and repeat with a third overlapping layer of pastry. Spoon the kale mixture into the pie dish, fold in the overhanging pieces of pastry and top with another two layers of pastry, brushing with butter between the layers. Finish with a final brush of melted butter.

Bake for 40 minutes or until the pie is golden brown and the base is cooked.

Remove the pie from the oven and let stand for 10 minutes before serving. I serve mine with a simple salad of greens from the garden.

SERVES 8

CHARRED LEEKS WITH YOGHURT AND CAPERS

Leeks are one of my favourite members of the Allium family. Fresh from the garden, they possess a subtle sweetness and are not as overpowering as onions or garlic. When they are split down the centre and finished on a chargrill they become all buttery, sweet and crisp, making this a great dish to add to your barbecue repertoire.

salt

4 leeks, scraggly roots and dark green stalks trimmed

olive oil, for brushing

black pepper

125 g (½ cup) natural Greek-style yoghurt

2 tablespoons baby capers, rinsed and dried

½ bunch of dill, fronds roughly chopped

70 g (½ cup) hazelnuts, lightly toasted and skins removed, roughly chopped

Fill a large saucepan with water and bring it to a rolling boil over high heat. Season the water generously with salt, enough to make it as salty as the sea.

Meanwhile, cut the leeks in half from root to tip, being sure to cut straight through the middle of the root mass (this will hold the leeks together during cooking). Give them a good wash to remove any remaining bits of dirt. Add the leeks to the boiling water and cook for 4 minutes or until tender when pressed with the tip of a knife but still maintaining their shape. Remove the leeks from the water and pat them dry with a clean tea towel.

Heat a chargrill pan over high heat. Brush the leeks with a little olive oil and place them, cut-side down, in the pan. Cook for 2–3 minutes or until they are starting to char nicely, then transfer them to a serving plate and season with a little salt and pepper.

Combine the yoghurt, capers and dill in a bowl, then spoon it over the leeks. Scatter over the hazelnuts and serve.

SERVES 4 AS A SIDE

CARAMELISED ONION AND LENTIL SOUP

This is a nourishing soup for your body and soul. It's earthy, sweet and hearty and will fill your home with an irresistible aroma as the onions gently caramelise. When the weather is grey and I'm feeling a bit lacklustre, this is the recipe I turn to.

olive oil, for cooking

1 kg onions, finely sliced

½ bunch of thyme, separated into sprigs

4 garlic cloves, finely sliced

1 litre beef stock

400 g can brown lentils, drained and rinsed

2 tablespoons red wine vinegar

salt and black pepper

buttered toasted sourdough, to serve

Heat a large saucepan over low heat and add a good splash of olive oil. Add the onion and thyme and cook as gently as possible for at least 30 minutes or until the onion has caramelised to a rich golden brown. This slow cooking is the backbone of the soup's flavour, so don't rush it!

Add the garlic and cook for another 5 minutes, then pour in the stock and stir in the lentils. Increase the heat to medium, bring the soup to a simmer and cook for another 10 minutes.

Just before serving, add the vinegar and season to taste with salt and pepper.

Ladle the soup into warm bowls and dish it up with slices of toasted sourdough, slathered in butter.

SERVES 8

PEA AND FETA FRITTERS WITH LABNEH

These sweet, salty fritters are an explosion of flavour, so I like to serve them simply with a few delicate leaves and some labneh. For those who haven't heard of it, labneh is yoghurt that has been drained to form a thick, tangy and almost cheese-like product. If you can't find any in the shops, you can easily make your own: line a sieve with a clean tea towel or piece of muslin and place it over a bowl, then spoon in some yoghurt and a pinch of salt. Let it drain in the fridge overnight then, hey presto! Homemade labneh.

400 g shelled peas (fresh is best but you could use frozen too)

salt

2 spring onions, green and white parts finely chopped

3 eggs, lightly beaten

100 g feta, finely crumbled

1 tablespoon plain flour

2 tablespoons roughly chopped mint leaves

2 tablespoons roughly chopped flat-leaf parsley leaves

black pepper

olive oil, for cooking and dressing

2 handfuls of sprouts or microgreens

200 g labneh

lemon wedges, to serve

Fill a medium saucepan with water, add a good pinch of salt and bring it to the boil over high heat. Plunge the peas into the boiling water and cook for 3 minutes or until tender, then drain well and place them in a large mixing bowl. Roughly mash the peas with a fork (I like to do mine about halfway between whole and pureed), then add the spring onion, egg, feta, flour, mint and parsley. Season with a little salt and pepper and mix gently to bring it all together.

Heat a large frying pan over medium heat and add a generous splash of olive oil. Plop a heaped tablespoon of the fritter mixture into the pan, then use the back of the spoon to flatten it into a 1 cm thick disc. Repeat until the pan is full but not overcrowded (you will probably need to cook the fritters in a couple of batches). Cook the fritters for 4 minutes on each side or until golden and cooked through, then pop them on a tray and cover to keep warm while you cook the rest. You should have about 20 fritters in all.

Lightly dress the sprouts or greens with olive oil. Divide the fritters among serving plates and serve with the labneh, sprouts or greens and lemon wedges for squeezing over.

SERVES 4

Pea and feta fritters with labneh

PEA, BARLEY AND HALOUMI SALAD

The sweetness of the peas contrasts beautifully with the saltiness of the haloumi in this salad. The addition of chewy, nutty barley rounds it out perfectly, making it delicious, nutritious and hearty.

140 g (⅔ cup) pearl barley, rinsed

500 ml (2 cups) vegetable stock

salt

310 g (2 cups) shelled peas

olive oil, for cooking and drizzling

360 g haloumi, cut into
1 cm thick slices

½ bunch of mint, leaves picked
and roughly torn

1 handful of pea shoots

juice of 1 lemon

black pepper

Combine the barley and stock in a medium saucepan and bring to the boil. Reduce the heat, pop a lid on the pan and simmer gently for 25–30 minutes or until the barley is tender, yet chewy. Remove the pan from the heat and leave to stand, covered, for 10 minutes, then take the lid off and fluff up the barley with a fork.

Fill a medium saucepan with water, add a good pinch of salt and bring it to the boil over high heat. Plunge the peas into the boiling water and cook for 3 minutes or until tender, then drain them well. Tip the peas into a large mixing bowl, add the barley and toss to combine.

Heat a large frying pan over medium–high heat and add a good splash of olive oil. Fry the haloumi for 2–3 minutes each side or until golden (depending on the size of your pan, you may need to do this in batches).

Add the haloumi to the barley mixture, along with the mint and pea shoots. Pour over the lemon juice and a little olive oil and season with salt and pepper. Gently toss to coat, then transfer to a serving dish and dig in while the haloumi is warm.

SERVES 4

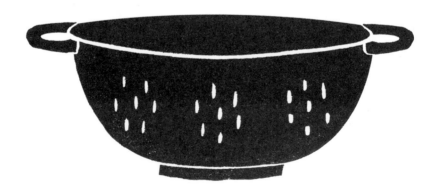

COOK VEGETABLES & FRUIT

POTATO AND LEMON
DRIZZLE CAKE

When someone mentions potato cake you tend to think of thin slices of potato, battered and deep-fried, but a sweet cake made from potato … whaaaaat? Truth is, potato is an excellent addition to a dense drizzle cake like this and it's the perfect recipe for those who don't like to bake with gluten. Everybody wins!

200 g unsalted butter

200 g caster sugar

4 eggs

200 g (2 cups) almond meal

200 g cold, very well mashed potato

2 teaspoons baking powder

finely grated zest of 2 lemons

natural Greek-style yoghurt or thick cream, to serve

LEMON SYRUP

juice of 2 lemons

60 g caster sugar

Preheat the oven to 160°C. Grease a 23 cm springform tin and line with baking paper.

Place the butter and sugar in the bowl of a stand mixer fitted with the paddle attachment and beat until light and fluffy. Add the eggs one at a time, beating between additions until they are well incorporated, then fold in the almond meal, mashed potato, baking powder and lemon zest.

Spoon the batter into the prepared tin and give the tin a couple of taps on the bench to level the batter out and smooth the surface. Bake for 45 minutes or until a skewer inserted in the centre comes out clean.

While the cake is baking, make the lemon syrup. Combine the lemon juice and sugar in a small saucepan and stir over medium heat just until the sugar has dissolved.

Remove the cake from the oven and prick it all over with a fork or bamboo skewer. Pour the hot syrup over the top, then let the cake cool in the tin for 10 minutes. Serve warm with a good dollop of natural yoghurt or cream.

SERVES 12

BUTTERNUT PUMPKIN HASH WITH FRIED EGGS

A good hash is my all-time favourite breakfast. Vegetables, herbs and crispy fried eggs – what's not to love? The pumpkin is perfect here as the little cubes become nicely caramelised while the insides stay meltingly tender.

olive oil, for cooking

1 onion, halved and finely sliced

1 small bunch of sage, leaves picked and roughly torn

1 small butternut pumpkin (about 1.5 kg), peeled, deseeded and cut into 2.5 cm cubes

50 g butter

½ bunch of flat-leaf parsley, leaves picked and roughly chopped

1 teaspoon dried chilli flakes

4 eggs

salt and black pepper

Heat a large heavy-based frying pan over medium heat and add a splash of olive oil. Pop the onion and sage in the pan and cook for a few minutes until the onion begins to turn translucent. Add the pumpkin and cook, stirring occasionally, for another 10 minutes or until the pumpkin is soft and starting to caramelise.

Add the butter to the pan. When it starts to foam and smell a little nutty, stir through the parsley and chilli flakes. Transfer the hash to four serving bowls.

Give the pan a quick clean and add a generous splash of olive oil, then return it to the stove and increase the heat to high. When the oil just starts to smoke, crack the eggs into the pan and reduce the heat to medium. This will give the eggs a nice crunchy base and then allow them to cook through. While they are cooking, spoon a little of the hot oil over the eggs or cover with a lid to make sure the whites set fully.

Remove the eggs from the pan and place one on each serve of hash. Season with salt and pepper and enjoy!

SERVES 4

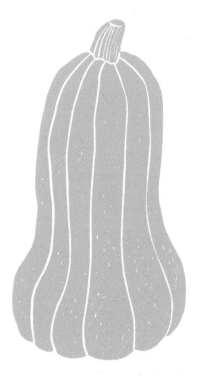

RHUBARB AND
COCONUT CRUMBLE

If you've never really been sure what to do with rhubarb this is the recipe you need to try. It's super simple to throw together and is made with ingredients you probably already have in your pantry. The baked rhubarb has an intoxicating aroma, but factor in the crunchy topping and vanilla ice cream and we're talking pure bliss!

1 bunch of rhubarb (about 500 g), trimmed, leaves removed and cut into 3 cm batons

3 tablespoons raw sugar

finely grated zest and juice of ½ lemon

vanilla ice cream, to serve

CRUMBLE TOPPING

50 g butter

80 g (⅓ cup) brown sugar

100 g (1 cup) rolled oats

30 g (½ cup) shredded coconut

Preheat the oven to 180°C and generously butter a 23 cm pie dish.

Place the rhubarb in a mixing bowl, add the raw sugar and the lemon zest and juice and give it all a good toss. Transfer the rhubarb to the prepared pie dish. Reserve the bowl to make the crumble.

To make the crumble topping, combine the butter and brown sugar in a small saucepan over medium heat and stir until the butter has melted and the sugar has dissolved. Pour the mixture into the bowl you used for the rhubarb, add the oats and coconut and mix well with a spoon. Spread the topping evenly over the rhubarb.

Pop the dish in the oven and bake for 30–35 minutes or until the crumble is golden brown and the rhubarb is bubbling underneath.

Remove the dish from the oven and stand for 10 minutes, then serve warm with big scoops of vanilla ice cream.

SERVES 4

RHUBARB, LEMON AND HONEY FOOL

It might sound like something Mr T would answer when asked to name his favourite vegetable, but in reality it's a healthy sweet treat that can be enjoyed for dessert, breakfast or as a tasty snack. So simple, but so good.

1 bunch of rhubarb (about 500 g), trimmed, leaves removed and cut into 2 cm batons

finely grated zest and juice of 1 lemon

2 tablespoons honey

500 g (2 cups) natural Greek-style yoghurt

80 g (½ cup) almonds, roughly chopped

a few sprigs of mint, leaves picked

edible flowers, to serve (optional)

Place the rhubarb, lemon zest and juice, honey and 125 ml (½ cup) of water in a deep saucepan over medium heat. Bring to the boil, then reduce the heat and simmer, covered, for 5 minutes or until the rhubarb is soft but still holding its shape. Remove from the heat and let the rhubarb cool completely.

To serve, spoon alternating layers of yoghurt and rhubarb into small glasses or bowls and top with the almonds and mint leaves. Finish with a sprinkling of edible flowers, if desired.

SERVES 4

Rhubarb, lemon and honey fool

SILVERBEET WITH SPICED CHICKPEAS AND ALMONDS

I absolutely love cooking this dish for lunch. It's filling without being heavy and is a great way to use one of the garden's most generous providers – good ol' silverbeet.

olive oil, for cooking

1 bunch of silverbeet (about 500 g), stalks removed and finely chopped, leaves shredded

1 onion, finely chopped

4 garlic cloves, finely chopped

1 long red chilli, finely chopped

1 teaspoon ground cumin

½ teaspoon cayenne pepper

½ teaspoon ground coriander

1 tablespoon tomato paste

400 g can chickpeas, drained and rinsed

finely grated zest and juice of 1 lemon

salt and black pepper

250 g (1 cup) natural Greek-style yoghurt

½ bunch of coriander, leaves picked and roughly torn

60 g (½ cup) slivered almonds, toasted

Heat a splash of olive oil in a deep heavy-based frying pan over medium heat. Toss in the silverbeet stalk and the onion and cook for 3 minutes or until softened. Add the garlic, chilli and ground spices and cook for another couple of minutes until aromatic.

Stir in the tomato paste and cook for another 2 minutes or until the paste has darkened and become aromatic. Pop the chickpeas and shredded silverbeet leaves in the pan and cook for 3 minutes or until the leaves have softened. Finally, stir in the lemon zest and juice and season to taste.

Spoon the silverbeet mixture into two bowls and top with yoghurt, coriander and almonds.

SERVES 2

STRAWBERRY AND VANILLA SEMIFREDDO

This is kind of like a cheat's ice cream that you don't have to churn. It's rich and creamy, and the strawberries impart an amazing perfume as well as a little tartness to offset the sweetness. The only catch is that you have to make it the night before you want to eat it so it has time to set.

250 g strawberries, hulled

3 eggs, separated

110 g (½ cup) caster sugar

1 vanilla bean, split and seeds scraped

400 ml thickened cream

GARNISH

250 g strawberries, hulled and quartered

1 tablespoon pure icing sugar

70 g (½ cup) shelled, unsalted pistachios, roughly chopped

Double-line a medium loaf tin with plastic wrap, making sure there is plenty of overhang.

Place the strawberries in the bowl of a food processor and blend until smooth. Combine the egg yolks, sugar and vanilla in a bowl and whisk until the mixture is pale and creamy. Set aside.

Place the egg whites in the scrupulously clean bowl of a stand mixer fitted with the whisk attachment and beat until they start to form very stiff peaks. Stop the mixer and place the bowl to one side.

In another bowl, whisk the cream until soft peaks form, then gently fold into the egg yolk mixture, along with the egg whites.

Spoon one-quarter of the cream mixture into the prepared tin and give the tin a gentle tap on the bench to level the mixture out, then spoon over one-quarter of the pureed strawberries. Repeat this layering with the remaining cream and strawberries, then fold over the overhanging plastic wrap to cover. Put the tin in the freezer overnight to set.

For the garnish, toss together the strawberries and icing sugar. Pop them in a covered container in the fridge to macerate overnight.

To serve, remove the tin from the freezer and peel back the plastic wrap. Gently turn out the semifreddo onto a bench and remove the plastic wrap altogether. Cut into 3 cm thick slices and place on cold plates. For the garnish, spoon over the macerated strawberries and finish with a sprinkling of pistachios.

SERVES 8

CREAMY SWEET POTATO AND LENTIL BAKE

This rich, delicious bake can be served as a side dish, or add a few fresh leaves from the garden and enjoy it as a meal in its own right. Arranging the discs of sweet potato upright in the dish not only looks spectacular, it makes the tops get all crispy while the bottom stays wonderfully creamy.

1.2 kg sweet potatoes

500 ml (2 cups) pouring cream

6 garlic cloves, finely sliced

400 g can brown lentils, drained and rinsed

salt and black pepper

½ bunch of thyme, separated into sprigs

80 g (½ cup) almonds, toasted and roughly chopped

Preheat the oven to 200°C.

Use a mandoline or a sharp knife to cut the sweet potato into 5 mm thick slices. Arrange the slices standing up in a deep baking dish.

Combine the cream, garlic and lentils in a medium saucepan and season with salt and pepper. Gently heat over low heat until the cream is just starting to steam. Carefully pour the cream mixture over the sweet potato, making sure the lentils are evenly distributed.

Scatter the thyme over the top, then cover the dish with foil and pop it in the oven for 45 minutes. Remove the foil and bake for a further 15 minutes or until the top is crisp and golden.

Remove from the oven and season with a pinch of salt. Scatter the almonds over the top and serve.

SERVES 6

REALLY GOOD HOMEMADE TOMATO SAUCE

Or, as it was known in my house when I was a kid, 'dead horse'.
I used to smother everything with it, and in those days it was pretty
much the only way Mum could get me to eat my veggies. We're all
so used to the stuff in the red bottle you buy at the supermarket that
making your own will be a revelation. Perfectly ripe tomatoes and
a few subtle spices give you a sauce that you'll want to slather over
everything, even as an adult!

4 kg ripe tomatoes, quartered and
core removed

2 onions, diced

8 garlic cloves, finely sliced

500 ml (2 cups) apple cider vinegar

2 teaspoons mustard seeds

1 teaspoon black peppercorns

1 teaspoon coriander seeds

440 g (2 cups) raw sugar

2 teaspoons sea salt

Place the tomato, onion and garlic in a large saucepan over medium
heat and bring to a simmer. Cook for about 30 minutes, stirring
occasionally, until everything is nice and soft.

Meanwhile, combine the vinegar, mustard seeds, peppercorns and
coriander seeds in a small saucepan over high heat. Bring to the boil,
then remove from the heat and leave the spices to infuse the vinegar
while the tomato mixture is cooking.

Run the softened tomato mixture through a food mill to remove the
skins and seeds. If you don't have a food mill, blitz it up in a food
processor, then pass it through a fine sieve.

Quickly wipe out the pan, then pour in the strained tomato sauce,
along with the sugar and salt. Strain the vinegar, discarding the spices,
and add it to the sauce. Place the pan over very low heat and simmer
gently for at least 2 hours or until it reaches a thick, saucy consistency.

Taste the sauce and adjust if necessary – you want a balance of sweet
and tangy with a hint of salt. When you're happy, transfer the sauce
to two 500 ml sterilised jars (see page 278), then wipe the rims and
seal. Left like this, the sauce will keep in the fridge for up to a month.

For a sauce that can be stored in the pantry for up to 2 years, the jars will
need to be heat treated. To do this, place a tea towel on the bottom of
a large saucepan that is deeper than the height of the jars and place the
jars on top, making sure they are not touching each other or the side of
the pan (this may cause them to crack during boiling).

Fill the saucepan with enough water to cover the jars, and bring it to
the boil. Boil for 15 minutes, then kill the heat and leave until the water
is cool enough for you to safely remove the jars. Wipe them dry, then
store them somewhere cool and dark for up to 2 years. Once opened,
store the jars in the fridge for up to a year.

MAKES 1 LITRE

TOMATO, BURRATA AND BASIL SALAD

There are few salads I enjoy more than one made with homegrown tomatoes still warm from the sun, pungent basil and fresh cheese. I've gone with burrata here because I love the way that gooey interior oozes out, covering everything else on the plate, but if you can't find it buffalo mozzarella or fresh curd will work well too.

1 large burrata

1 kg mixed tomatoes, small ones halved, larger ones cut into 1 cm thick slices

2 tablespoons baby capers, rinsed and dried

80 ml (⅓ cup) olive oil, plus extra for brushing

1½ tablespoons red wine vinegar

salt and black pepper

1 bunch of basil, leaves picked

sliced sourdough, to serve (optional)

Place the burrata in the centre of a serving platter and arrange the tomato around it. Scatter the capers over the tomato.

Whisk together the olive oil and vinegar and drizzle it over the tomato. Season generously with salt and pepper, then roughly tear the basil leaves over the top.

If you would like to serve the salad with sourdough, heat a chargrill pan over high heat. Brush the sourdough slices with olive oil, then add to the pan and cook on both sides until nice char lines appear.

Just before serving, slice the burrata open – the creamy interior will ooze out over the tomatoes. Serve immediately with some sourdough, if desired, for mopping up all of the deliciousness.

SERVES 4 AS A SIDE

CHARGRILLED WATERMELON WITH CHILLI, LIME AND MINT

This is something a little different to try next time you have a watermelon and a hot barbecue nearby. Searing the melon adds a smoky layer of flavour that contrasts with its natural sweetness. The freshness of the mint finishes the dish perfectly.

olive oil, for brushing

2 kg watermelon, cut into 2 cm thick wedges

2 teaspoons caster sugar

2 teaspoons sea salt

1 teaspoon dried chilli flakes

2 limes, zested then cut into wedges

1 bunch of mint, leaves picked

250 g (1 cup) natural Greek-style yoghurt

Give your chargrill pan a really good clean and brush lightly with olive oil, then heat it over high heat.

Brush the watermelon wedges with a tiny bit of olive oil, then combine the sugar, salt, chilli and lime zest and sprinkle it evenly over both sides of the watermelon.

Grill the watermelon wedges for 3 minutes on each side or until nicely charred. Remove from the grill and arrange on a serving platter.

Scatter over the mint and serve with the yoghurt and lime wedges.

SERVES 4

WATERMELON GRANITA

I first tried watermelon granita on a sweltering summer's day in Melbourne. I stumbled into a coffee shop for a rejuvenating shot of espresso and the waiter was scooping this amazing-looking pink ice out of a tub for some experienced-looking patrons. Curiosity got the better of me and I ordered a scoop for myself – wow! To this day I'm yet to find a more refreshing treat to enjoy on a blasting hot day.

220 g (1 cup) caster sugar

2 kg watermelon

juice of 1 lemon

shredded mint, to garnish

Combine the sugar and 250 ml (1 cup) water in a saucepan over medium heat and stir until the sugar has dissolved. Remove the pan from the heat and set aside.

Remove the rind from the watermelon and roughly chop the flesh so you can put it in the bowl of a food processor. Puree the watermelon, then pour in the sugar syrup and lemon juice and blend until smooth and well combined.

Pour the mixture into a couple of clean baking trays, then pop them in the freezer. Come back every hour or so and scrape with a fork to break up the ice crystals that have formed. Repeat this four to five times until you have a fluffy, icy consistency.

To serve, spoon the granita into bowls, garnish with mint and enjoy as an icy respite from a hot day in the garden.

SERVES 8

ZUCCHINI AND CHOCOLATE CAKE

I'd like to say that including zucchini in this cake automatically makes it a health food but unfortunately that would be a lie. It is, however, an incredibly delicious way to use up all the zucchini that seem to relentlessly appear in the garden at the height of summer.

120 g (1 cup) spelt flour

1 teaspoon baking powder

3 tablespoons cocoa powder

115 g (½ cup) brown sugar

pinch of salt

2 eggs

125 ml (½ cup) olive oil

2 zucchini (about 400 g), grated

170 g (1 cup) dark choc chips

30 g (½ cup) flaked coconut, toasted

CHOCOLATE ICING

125 g unsalted butter, softened

60 g (½ cup) icing sugar

60 g (½ cup) cocoa powder

1 tablespoon milk, if needed

Preheat the oven to 160°C. Grease a medium loaf tin and line with baking paper.

Sift the flour, baking powder and cocoa powder into a large mixing bowl, then add the brown sugar and salt.

In a separate bowl, whisk together the eggs and olive oil, then fold them into the dry ingredients with a spatula. Add the zucchini and choc chips and fold in until well combined.

Spoon the batter into the prepared tin and give it a couple of good taps on the bench to remove any air pockets. Bake for 1 hour or until a skewer inserted in the centre comes out clean. Remove from the oven and let the cake cool in the tin for 10 minutes or so, then turn out onto a wire rack to cool completely.

Meanwhile, make the chocolate icing. Pop the butter in the bowl of a stand mixer fitted with the paddle attachment. Sift in the icing sugar and cocoa powder and beat until smooth. If the mixture is a little thick, gradually add the milk until the icing is the right consistency.

Spread the icing over the cooled cake and finish with the coconut. Store in an airtight container at room temperature for up to 5 days.

SERVES 10

GRILLED ZUCCHINI WITH
GOAT'S CHEESE, HERBS AND HAZELNUTS

When the weather gets warm, my garden starts pumping out zucchini faster than I can cook them! This salad is made for summer barbecuing, whether you whip it up as a simple lunch or let it shine as a flavour-packed side dish. You can easily double or triple the quantities if you are feeding a crowd.

olive oil, for cooking

2 zucchini, thickly sliced lengthways

salt

100 g goat's cheese, crumbled

140 g (1 cup) hazelnuts, lightly toasted and skins removed, roughly chopped

½ bunch of flat-leaf parsley, leaves picked and roughly chopped

½ bunch of mint, leaves picked and roughly chopped

DRESSING

3 tablespoons olive oil

1 tablespoon apple cider vinegar

1 teaspoon dijon mustard

Heat a chargrill pan or heavy-based frying pan over high heat. Add a splash of olive oil, then add the zucchini slices in a single layer and sprinkle over a bit of salt. Cook the zucchini for about 2 minutes each side – you want it to be cooked through and have a nice brown crust. Remove the zucchini from the pan and drain on paper towel, then arrange it on a serving plate.

To make the dressing, whisk together all the ingredients in a small bowl or give them a shake in a little jar.

To serve, scatter the goat's cheese, hazelnuts, parsley and mint over the zucchini and drizzle over the dressing to finish.

SERVES 2 AS A MAIN OR 4 AS A SIDE

MEAT.

CHICKEN: Chicken and garden greens soup; Barbecued butterflied chicken with green tahini sauce; Chicken pot roast to feed a family **PORK:** Roast pork belly with quick pickled radish; Smoked pork hock and cabbage soup **LAMB:** Slow-cooked lamb shanks with spiced chickpeas; Lamb breast stuffed with lemon and herbs; Simple lamb liver pate; Spiced lamb shoulder with turmeric rice pilaf; Rosemary lamb ribs with chilli salt and lemon; Lamb chops braised with wine and cannellini beans **BEEF:** Smoky beef brisket with sweet and spicy barbecue sauce; Flank steak with fresh salsa and fat chips; Beef heart and mushroom skewers; Braised beef shin with chilli and beans; Marinated skirt steak tacos; Whisky-braised beef short ribs

CHICKEN AND GARDEN GREENS SOUP

This is one of my favourite things to cook in spring. I always have a good stand of silverbeet in my garden at this time of year, and this light, clear broth is exactly what I crave when the weather is slowly starting to warm up but winter hasn't yet released its icy grip.

2 carrots, finely diced

1 bunch of silverbeet
(about 500 g), stalks and
leaves finely shredded

6 garlic cloves, finely sliced

400 g can brown lentils, drained
and rinsed

1 bunch of flat-leaf parsley,
leaves picked and torn

salt and black pepper

BROTH

1 × 1.5 kg free-range chicken

1 onion, chopped

1 carrot, chopped

1 celery stalk, chopped

1 tablespoon apple cider vinegar

½ bunch of thyme, separated
into sprigs

2 bay leaves

10 black peppercorns

To make the broth, place all the ingredients in a large saucepan and pour in 3 litres of water. Bring to the boil over high heat, then reduce the heat to low and let it gently bubble away for 1½ hours or until the chicken is cooked and the meat is easy to shred.

Remove the chicken with a large slotted spoon and place it on a plate to cool.

Strain the broth through a fine sieve, discarding the solids. Return the broth to the pan and add the carrot, silverbeet, garlic and lentils. Bring to the boil over high heat, then reduce the heat and simmer for 5 minutes.

Meanwhile, remove the chicken meat from the bones and pull it apart with your fingers.

Add the shredded chicken and parsley to the soup and give it all a good stir. Check the seasoning and add a little salt and pepper if desired, then ladle it into serving bowls and serve.

SERVES 6

COOK MEAT

BARBECUED BUTTERFLIED CHICKEN WITH GREEN TAHINI SAUCE

Who said the only way you can cook a whole chook is by roasting it? I love the charred flavours I get by chargrilling a butterflied chicken. To butterfly the chicken, place it on a board, breast side down, and use sharp kitchen scissors to cut out a 3 cm strip from the back to the front. This strip is the chicken's back bone and when you remove it you should be able to open up the cavity and push the carcass flat. You'll need to start this recipe a day in advance – the brining is essential to stop the meat from drying out during cooking.

1 × 1.5 kg free-range chicken, butterflied

1 lemon, cut into wedges

BRINE

130 g (1 cup) sea salt

230 g (1 cup) caster sugar

1 teaspoon coriander seeds

1 teaspoon cumin seeds

1 teaspoon black peppercorns

½ bunch of thyme, separated into sprigs

2 bay leaves

GREEN TAHINI SAUCE

salt

1 bunch of flat-leaf parsley, leaves picked

1 bunch of mint, leaves picked

1 bunch of coriander, leaves picked

135 g (½ cup) tahini

250 ml (1 cup) olive oil

juice of 1 lemon, or to taste

black pepper

To prepare the brine, pour 4 litres of water into a large saucepan and bring to the boil. Add the salt and sugar and stir until dissolved. Remove from the heat and allow to cool to room temperature, then stir in the spices and herbs.

Add the butterflied chicken to the cooled brine, making sure the chicken is completely submerged (you may need to use a plate to weigh it down). Pop the pan in the fridge and refrigerate overnight.

The next day, remove the chicken from the brine and pat dry with a clean tea towel. Put the chicken on a plate and return to the fridge, uncovered, for at least a couple of hours to dry out the skin. Remove the chicken from the fridge an hour before cooking to allow the meat to come to room temperature.

To make the green tahini sauce, bring a saucepan of lightly salted water to the boil and add the herbs. Blanch for a few seconds, then refresh in iced water to stop the cooking process. Remove the herbs from the water and squeeze out as much liquid as possible. Transfer to a blender, add the tahini, olive oil and lemon juice and blend until smooth. Season with salt and pepper and more lemon juice if needed.

Preheat a barbecue grill to medium or a chargrill pan over medium heat. Add the chicken, skin-side down, and cook for about 10 minutes or until the skin is nicely brown and crispy. Reduce the heat to low, turn the bird over and cook for 20–30 minutes or until the meat is cooked through. The best way to tell if the chicken is cooked is to use a meat thermometer – you're looking for a reading of 75°C. If you don't have a thermometer, pierce the flesh in the thickest part – if the juices run clear, it's ready. Remove the chicken from the grill, cover with foil and place somewhere warm to rest for 15 minutes.

Give the lemon wedges a quick grill to develop the flavour and add a bit of colour. Place the chicken on a serving plate, skin-side up, drizzle over the tahini sauce and serve with the grilled lemon wedges.

SERVES 6

CHICKEN POT ROAST
TO FEED A FAMILY

A pot roast is a super simple way to cook up a richly flavoured and nutritious feed. You're essentially making a stock and dinner in one recipe here, and the root veggies round it out nicely.

olive oil, for cooking

1 × 1.5 kg free-range chicken

200 g flat pancetta, cut into batons

1 onion, sliced

2 carrots, sliced

2 celery stalks, sliced

1 head of garlic, halved horizontally

500 ml (2 cups) white wine

½ bunch of thyme, separated into sprigs

1 bay leaf

10 black peppercorns

8–10 small new potatoes, washed and halved

½ bunch baby turnips (about 250 g), trimmed and halved

½ bunch radishes (about 250 g), trimmed and halved

salt and black pepper

green salad, bread and dijon mustard, to serve

Choose a saucepan large enough to snugly fit the whole chicken. Add a splash of olive oil and heat over high heat, then add the chicken and brown it all over as best you can. Remove and set aside.

Add the pancetta to the pan and cook until nicely browned, then add the onion, carrot, celery and garlic and cook for another 5 minutes or until softened. Deglaze the pan with the white wine, scraping up any bits caught on the bottom, then pop the chicken back in. Top with enough water to fully cover the chicken and add the thyme, bay leaf and peppercorns. Bring the liquid to the boil, then reduce the heat and simmer, covered, for 1 hour.

Add the potatoes and turnips and cook for 20 minutes, then add the radishes and cook for a further 10 minutes. By now, the chicken and all the vegetables should be cooked through. Check the seasoning and add a little salt and pepper if desired.

Remove the chicken from the broth with a slotted spoon and either shred the meat or roughly break it into portions.

Spoon the vegetables and broth into bowls and top with the chicken meat. Serve with a fresh green salad, bread and dijon mustard.

SERVES 6

ROAST PORK BELLY WITH QUICK PICKLED RADISH

Pork belly is such an amazing cut of meat, and when you get that crackling right, PHWOAR! I leave my pork belly uncovered, skin-side up, in the fridge for at least 12 hours before I cook it. The low-humidity environment of the fridge draws out any excess moisture in the skin, which is the key to earth-shattering crackling.

2 kg boneless pork belly, skin on

1 tablespoon fennel seeds

salt

olive oil, for cooking

6 onions, cut into wedges

2 turnips, cut into wedges

½ bunch of thyme, separated into sprigs

PICKLED RADISH

1 bunch of radishes (about 16), halved or cut into wedges

100 ml red wine vinegar

1 tablespoon caster sugar

1 teaspoon black peppercorns

1 teaspoon coriander seeds

The day before you want to eat, remove any wrapping from the pork and leave it uncovered in the fridge – this helps to dry the skin, leading to amazing crackling.

When you are ready to cook, remove the pork from the fridge and let it come to room temperature.

Preheat the oven to 220°C.

Toast the fennel seeds in a dry frying pan over medium heat until aromatic, then roughly grind them with a mortar and pestle.

Use a sharp knife to score the skin of the pork belly, then massage the fennel seeds into the cuts and skin, along with some salt and olive oil. Arrange the onion, turnip and thyme sprigs in a large roasting tin, pour over 1 litre of water and sit the pork on top. Place the tin in the oven and roast for 15 minutes or until the skin starts to bubble. Reduce the temperature to 170°C and roast for another 1½–2 hours or until the meat is cooked through and the crackling is golden and super crunchy. Remove from the oven and rest for 15 minutes.

Meanwhile, to make the pickled radish, place the radish in a glass or ceramic bowl. Combine the vinegar, sugar, peppercorns and coriander seeds in a saucepan and stir over high heat until the sugar has dissolved. Pour the hot liquid over the radishes and place to one side until you are ready to serve.

Cut the pork into slices as thick or as thin as you like and serve with the roast vegetables and pickled radish.

SERVES 8

SMOKED PORK HOCK AND CABBAGE SOUP

This is my ultimate comfort food. There's nothing better than waking up on a bleak winter's day and popping this soup on to simmer while you go about your daily chores. The smoked hock adds an incredible depth of flavour, and the big dollop of sour cream at the end sets the whole thing off perfectly.

olive oil, for cooking

1 head of garlic, cloves peeled and sliced

1 onion, finely sliced

1 carrot, diced

2 potatoes, diced

½ white cabbage, cored and finely shredded

1 kg smoked pork hock

3 litres chicken stock or water

salt and black pepper, if needed

200 g sour cream

½ bunch of flat-leaf parsley, leaves picked and finely chopped

Heat a very large saucepan over medium heat and add a splash of olive oil. Add the garlic, onion, carrot, potato and cabbage and cook for 5 minutes or until softened. Add the hock, pour in the stock or water and bring to the boil, then reduce the heat to low and simmer gently for 1–1½ hours or until the meat falls easily off the bone. Remove the pan from the heat.

Using a slotted spoon, remove the hock from the liquid and set aside to cool. Peel off and thinly slice the skin, and shred the meat off the bone using your fingers. Return the skin and meat to the soup, reheat if necessary and check the seasoning – the smoked pork will make it quite salty so you'll probably only need a pinch of pepper.

To serve, ladle the soup into warm bowls, top with generous dollop of sour cream and finish with a scattering of parsley.

SERVES 6

SLOW-COOKED LAMB SHANKS
WITH SPICED CHICKPEAS

Good ol' lamb shanks. As far as secondary cuts go, this is one of the most familiar. Unfortunately, that familiarity has forced the price up a bit over the years, but it is still an affordable cut that is easy to cook and big on flavour. Paired here with Middle Eastern spices and chickpeas, this is a dish that will fill your house with exotic aromas and fill your belly with delicious hearty fare.

olive oil, for cooking

4 lamb shanks

salt and black pepper

2 red onions, finely sliced

2 tablespoons garam masala

500 ml (2 cups) chicken stock

400 g can crushed tomatoes

400 g can chickpeas, drained and rinsed

½ bunch of thyme, separated into sprigs

2 bay leaves

125 g (½ cup) natural Greek-style yoghurt

2 handfuls of rocket leaves

Preheat the oven to 160°C.

Heat a large flameproof casserole dish over medium heat and add a good splash of olive oil. Season the lamb shanks liberally with salt and pepper, then add them to the pan and cook for 5 minutes or until they are browned all over. Remove and set aside.

Add a little more olive oil to the dish and cook the onion for 5 minutes, then sprinkle in the garam masala and cook for another 2 minutes. Add the stock, crushed tomatoes, chickpeas, thyme and bay leaves. Nestle the lamb shanks into the chickpea mixture, then bring the whole lot to a simmer. Cover with a tight-fitting lid and pop it all in the oven for 2–3 hours or until the meat is so tender it falls easily off the bone.

To serve, spoon the chickpea mixture into four bowls and carefully place the shanks on top. Spoon some yoghurt over the top and finish with the rocket leaves.

SERVES 4

LAMB BREAST STUFFED WITH LEMON AND HERBS

Lamb breast is another underappreciated, cheap cut of meat. It's like the lamb version of pork belly, but is much smaller and thinner, which is why I roll it up with fresh herbs and mustard. If you've never rolled a piece of meat before, this is a great one to start with. Don't worry too much about any fancy knot work – as long as it kind of holds its shape, it'll be just fine.

1 boneless lamb breast (about 1 kg)

salt and black pepper

1 tablespoon dijon mustard

olive oil, for cooking

1 onion, finely diced

4 garlic cloves, finely chopped

½ bunch of flat-leaf parsley, leaves picked and finely chopped

1 rosemary sprig, leaves picked and finely chopped

finely grated zest of 1 lemon

green salad, to serve

Preheat the oven to 150°C.

Place the lamb breast, skin-side down, on a large chopping board and use a sharp knife to score the meat in a cross-hatch pattern. Season generously with salt and pepper, then rub the mustard into the meat.

Heat a large frying pan over medium heat and add a splash of olive oil. Add the onion and garlic and cook gently for 5 minutes or until softened, then spoon it evenly over the lamb breast. Wipe out the pan (you'll need it later to brown the lamb).

Mix together the parsley, rosemary and lemon zest and spoon it over the onion.

Starting with one of the long sides, roll up the lamb breast into a tight sausage shape, then secure it with kitchen string at 5 cm intervals. Place the pan you used for the onion mixture over medium–high heat and add a splash of olive oil. Fry the lamb breast for 5–7 minutes or until nicely browned all over.

Transfer the lamb to a roasting tin, pop it in the oven and cook for 1½ hours or until cooked through. Cut into slices and serve with a fresh green salad.

SERVES 4

SIMPLE LAMB LIVER PATE

I love pate – smooth and buttery, with that subtle meaty flavour that liver is so good for. This is another cut that you'll have to visit a butcher for, but it's cheap, incredibly nutritious and so easy to cook. Just be sure to err on the side of undercooking so it's still nice and pink in the middle; overcook it and your pate will have an undesirable mealy texture.

olive oil, for cooking

1 lamb's liver

1 golden shallot, finely diced

1 bunch of thyme, leaves picked

75 ml brandy

100 g butter, at room temperature

75 ml double cream

salt and black pepper

crusty bread, to serve

Heat a frying pan over medium–high heat, add a splash of olive oil and fry the liver until browned but still pink in the centre – this should only take about 2 minutes each side. Remove the liver to a plate or board. Add another splash of olive oil to the pan and cook the shallot and thyme for 2 minutes or until soft and aromatic. Add the brandy and cook for another minute.

Transfer the mixture to the bowl of a food processor, along with the liver, and blend until combined. Add the butter and cream and a little salt and pepper and continue blending until smooth.

Scoop the pate into a bowl and enjoy immediately with some crusty bread. If you don't eat it all in one sitting it will keep, covered, in the fridge for up to 3 days.

SERVES 8

SPICED LAMB SHOULDER
WITH TURMERIC RICE PILAF

Lamb shoulder is my favourite cut of meat for feeding a crowd.
I always order it with bone in, so that as it cooks the bone adds
an extra depth of flavour. In this recipe the lamb is richly spiced,
and I like to serve it with a simple rice pilaf as a meal that can be
enjoyed for lunch or dinner, even when the weather is warm.

2 onions, roughly chopped

500 ml (2 cups) chicken stock

2.5 kg lamb shoulder, bone in

olive oil, for drizzling

1 tablespoon ground cumin

1 tablespoon ground coriander

salt and black pepper

400 g natural Greek-style yoghurt

1 bunch of coriander, leaves
picked and roughly torn

lemon wedges, to serve

TURMERIC RICE PILAF

olive oil, for cooking

1 onion, finely diced

1 teaspoon ground turmeric

1 teaspoon sumac

400 g (2 cups) basmati rice,
thoroughly rinsed under cold water

750 ml (3 cups) chicken stock

130 g (1 cup) dried cranberries

45 g (½ cup) flaked almonds,
lightly toasted

Preheat the oven to 160°C.

To make the rice pilaf, place a flameproof casserole dish over medium heat and add a good splash of olive oil. Add the onion and cook, stirring occasionally, for 3 minutes, then sprinkle in the turmeric and sumac and cook for a further 2 minutes. Add the rice and give everything a good stir so the rice is well coated with the oil and spices, then pour in the stock and bring it to the boil. Remove the dish from the heat, cover with a tight-fitting lid and pop it in the oven for 45 minutes. Remove the cooked rice from the oven and spread it out on a tray, then place it in the fridge to cool. Once cold, transfer to a container with a lid and keep it in the fridge until just before you are ready to serve.

A few hours before you want to eat, preheat the oven to 220°C.

Combine the onion and chicken stock in a casserole dish, then place the lamb shoulder on top. Drizzle olive oil all over the shoulder, then use your hands to rub in the cumin and coriander, as well as plenty of salt and pepper. Place the dish in the oven (without the lid) and cook for 30 minutes.

Reduce the oven temperature to 150°C, cover the dish with a tight-fitting lid and cook for a further 2–3 hours or until the meat falls easily off the bone.

To finish the rice pilaf, combine the cold rice with the dried cranberries and flaked almonds.

Shred the meat using two forks, then divide the pilaf and lamb among serving plates. Top with yoghurt and coriander and serve with lemon wedges for squeezing over.

SERVES 6–8

Spiced lamb shoulder with turmeric rice pilaf

ROSEMARY LAMB RIBS WITH
CHILLI SALT AND LEMON

This is my ultimate snack food. Any time there's a big sporting event on and I'm catching up with a few mates to watch it, I knock out a batch of these. Tender in the middle, crispy on the outside and with a chilli kick from the salt, these bad boys are a winner every time, even if my team isn't.

1.5 kg lamb ribs, cut into single-bone cutlets

salt and black pepper

1 head of garlic, halved horizontally

4 rosemary sprigs

500 ml (2 cups) white wine

lemon wedges, to serve

CHILLI SALT

2 tablespoons sea salt

2 teaspoons dried chilli flakes

1 teaspoon smoked paprika

Preheat the oven to 150°C.

Season the lamb ribs generously with salt and pepper and place them in a deep roasting tin, along with the garlic, rosemary and wine. Cover the lamb ribs with a sheet of baking paper, then tightly cover the tin with foil. Place in the oven and cook for 1½ hours or until the meat is very tender.

Preheat a grill to high. Transfer the ribs to a baking tray and grill them for 5 minutes or until golden brown and crispy.

Meanwhile, to make the chilli salt, combine all the ingredients in a small bowl.

To serve, arrange the ribs on a serving platter, sprinkle over the chilli salt and serve with lemon wedges.

SERVES 4

LAMB CHOPS BRAISED WITH WINE AND CANNELLINI BEANS

Forget those fancy lamb cutlets – a good forequarter chop wins me over every time. The meat is flavoursome and fatty, and imparts a lovely richness to this slow-cooked dish. The beans work particularly well here, soaking up all the flavours and making the dish as hearty as it is appetising.

olive oil, for cooking

4 lamb forequarter chops

salt and black pepper

1 onion, finely sliced

2 celery stalks, finely sliced

1 rosemary sprig, leaves picked and finely chopped

250 ml (1 cup) white wine

400 g can cannellini beans, drained and rinsed

1 bunch of flat-leaf parsley, leaves picked

Preheat the oven to 150°C.

Heat a large flameproof casserole dish over medium heat and add a good splash of olive oil. Season the lamb chops generously with salt and pepper, then fry for 2–3 minutes each side or until nicely browned. Remove them from the dish. Reduce the heat to low and add a little more olive oil to the dish, then pop in the onion, celery and rosemary and cook for 5 minutes or until softened.

Add the wine and beans, increase the heat to high and bring the mixture to a simmer. Return the lamb to the dish, then cover with a tight-fitting lid and pop the dish in the oven. Cook for 1–1½ hours or until the lamb is nice and tender.

Remove the lamb chops and stir the parsley into the bean mixture.

To serve, spoon the braised beans into shallow bowls and top with the lamb chops.

SERVES 4

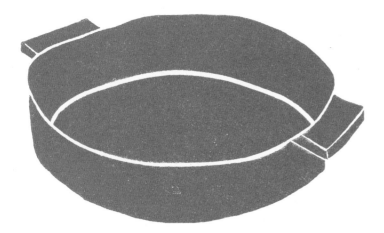

SMOKY BEEF BRISKET WITH SWEET AND SPICY BARBECUE SAUCE

This is a recipe for those of you who love the flavour of American-style barbecue, but don't want to spend the coin on buying a smoker or aren't prepared to stand by a fire all night. The brisket here is super juicy and the smoked paprika fills in where a smoker is lacking. Cooking this may not earn you the title of 'pitmaster' but it will be sure to please anyone who sits down to eat it!

2 kg beef brisket

1 tablespoon sea salt

1 tablespoon smoked paprika

1 tablespoon freshly ground black pepper

500 ml (2 cups) beef stock

small gherkins, to serve

green salad, to serve

BARBECUE SAUCE

olive oil, for cooking

1 onion, finely diced

2 garlic cloves, finely chopped

1 teaspoon cayenne pepper

2 tablespoons tomato paste

400 g can crushed tomatoes

125 ml (½ cup) malt vinegar

3 tablespoons molasses

Preheat the oven to 180°C.

Place the brisket on a large chopping board. Combine the salt, paprika and pepper in a bowl, then rub the mixture all over the beef. Place the beef in a large roasting tin, fat-side up, and pop in the oven to roast for 1 hour.

Remove the tin from the oven and reduce the temperature to 150°C. Pour the stock into the tin. Cover the brisket with baking paper and cover the tray with foil, then return to the oven for a further 2 hours.

Meanwhile, prepare the barbecue sauce. Pour a splash of olive oil into a medium saucepan and heat over medium heat. Add the onion and garlic and cook for 5 minutes or until softened, then sprinkle over the cayenne pepper and cook for another 2 minutes. Add the tomato paste and cook for 3–5 minutes, stirring regularly, then reduce the heat to low and add the tomatoes, vinegar and molasses. Cook for about 15 minutes or until the sauce has thickened.

After the brisket has been roasting for about 2 hours, remove the foil and baking paper and brush some of the barbecue sauce over the beef, then put it back in the oven for a further 15–30 minutes or until golden brown and cooked through. Remove it from the oven and let it rest somewhere warm for 15 minutes or so.

Carve the beef across the grain into 5 mm thick slices and top with the remaining barbecue sauce. Serve with some gherkins and a fresh green salad.

SERVES 8

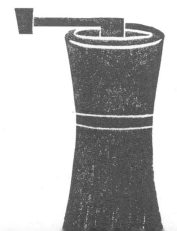

FLANK STEAK WITH FRESH SALSA AND FAT CHIPS

The great thing about flank is that, while it's considered a secondary cut, it's still tender enough to be quickly grilled. The flank comes from the bottom of the abdominal region of the cow, and has a pronounced grain and strong beefy flavour. It's highly regarded as a grilling cut in South America and goes down a treat here with some homemade chips and a fresh, tangy salsa.

500 g nicola or dutch cream potatoes

salt

800 g tallow or 800 ml sunflower oil

2 × 500 g beef flank steaks

black pepper

FRESH SALSA

2 avocados, flesh roughly chopped

1 bunch of coriander, leaves picked and roughly chopped

250 g cherry tomatoes, halved

½ red onion, finely sliced

juice of 1 lemon

1 long red chilli, finely sliced

salt and black pepper

Peel the potatoes if you like (personally, I don't bother) and cut them into chunky chips. Rinse under cold water, then immediately drop them into a saucepan of cold salted water. Bring to the boil, then reduce the heat and gently simmer for 10 minutes or until a knife can be pushed through the potato with little resistance. Use a slotted spoon to remove the chips from the water and gently shake off any excess moisture. Arrange them in a single layer on a baking tray and leave them to steam-dry.

Place the tallow or oil in a large heavy-based saucepan and heat over medium–high heat to 140°C. If you don't have a thermometer, place the handle of a wooden spoon in the oil – it should bubble gently. Add the potato chips and blanch until they are cooked through but not coloured, about 3 minutes. Remove them from the tallow or oil with a slotted spoon and drain on paper towel.

To make the salsa, place all the ingredients in a bowl and gently toss to combine.

Generously season the steak with salt and pepper. Heat a heavy-based frying pan or chargrill pan over medium–high heat, add the steaks and cook for 2–3 minutes each side. Remove from the pan and allow to rest for a few minutes.

Heat the tallow or oil again, this time to 180°C or until the handle of a wooden spoon bubbles constantly but not vigorously. Add the chips and cook for 5 minutes or until they are crunchy and golden brown. Remove with a slotted spoon and drain on paper towel, then season generously with salt.

To serve, slice the steak and spoon the salsa over the top. Serve the chips on the side.

SERVES 4

BEEF HEART AND MUSHROOM SKEWERS

Beef heart is the offal for people who don't like offal. It has a similar texture to a regular cut of beef and its flavour is 'beefy' without being too 'offaly'. You'll need to visit your butcher for this one and purchase a whole heart, which is a little large for this recipe, so use half, then wrap the rest and freeze it for next time. Because it is a muscle that is constantly working, the heart benefits from being marinated and cooked quickly over high heat.

½ beef heart

1 red onion

250 g button mushrooms, quartered

olive oil, for brushing

MARINADE

4 garlic cloves, finely chopped

1 teaspoon smoked paprika

3 tablespoons olive oil

Soak 10–12 wooden skewers in water for 20 minutes or so before using so they don't burn during cooking.

Separate the heart into chambers and trim away any fat, gristle or membrane. Finely slice the heart and place in a glass or ceramic dish.

To make the marinade, combine all the ingredients in a bowl. Pour it over the heart and gently mix. Set aside in the fridge to marinate for at least 30 minutes or overnight if you have time.

Cut the onion into wedges and separate the layers. Thread the heart onto the skewers, alternating with pieces of mushroom and onion.

Heat a large chargrill pan or barbecue to medium–high.

Lightly brush the skewers with oil, then add to the pan or barbecue and cook for 2–3 minutes each side or until the heart is medium–rare.

SERVES 4

BRAISED BEEF SHIN
WITH CHILLI AND BEANS

You've no doubt heard of or even used beef shin under its other name 'osso bucco'. As the name clearly suggests, it's the thickly sliced shin of a cow and is a fantastic cut of beef for slow cooking. The presence of the bone and marrow make for an incredibly rich and nutritious braise. This recipe takes a little bit of effort and a whole lot of time but rewards you with fall-apart meat and a flavour-packed sauce.

olive oil, for cooking

6–8 pieces (about 1.5 kg) beef shin (osso bucco)

salt and black pepper

2 red onions, finely sliced

2 long red chillies, finely sliced

1 tablespoon smoked paprika

1 tablespoon ground cumin

1 tablespoon dried oregano

500 ml (2 cups) beef stock

400 g can crushed tomatoes

400 g can Mexican bean mix

400 g sour cream

½ bunch of coriander, leaves picked and roughly torn

lime wedges, to serve

Preheat the oven to 150°C.

Place a large flameproof casserole dish over medium heat and add a good splash of olive oil. Generously season the beef with salt and pepper, then add it to the dish and cook for 3–4 minutes each side or until nicely browned. Remove the beef and set aside.

Add a little more olive oil to the dish, then pop in the onion and chilli and cook, stirring occasionally, for 5 minutes or until softened. Add the paprika, cumin and oregano and cook for another 2–3 minutes. Return the beef to the pan, placing it on top of the onion mixture, then add the stock, tomatoes and beans. Bring the whole lot to a simmer, then cover with a tight-fitting lid and transfer the dish to the oven. Cook for 2–3 hours or until the beef is meltingly tender.

To serve, spoon the beef and beans into bowls, top with sour cream and coriander and finish with a squeeze of lime juice.

SERVES 6–8

MARINATED SKIRT STEAK TACOS

Skirt steak is a long fibrous muscle that comes from the diaphragm of a cow. It's a little tougher and 'beefier' than flank steak so benefits from an overnight marinade. After removing the steak from the marinade and bringing it back to room temperature, the meat is best cooked quickly over high heat. If you like your steak well done, this isn't the cut for you.

500 g skirt steak

8 corn tortillas

2 avocados, flesh thickly sliced

½ red onion, finely sliced

½ bunch of coriander, leaves picked

Fermented Hot Chilli Sauce (page 162) or your other favourite chilli sauce, to serve

lime wedges, to serve

MARINADE

juice of 1 lime

1 tablespoon finely chopped coriander root

2 garlic cloves, finely chopped

1 teaspoon ground cumin

1 teaspoon cayenne pepper

100 ml olive oil

To make the marinade, combine all the ingredients in a glass or ceramic dish. Add the steak and turn to coat well, then cover and marinate in the fridge for as long as you can, up to 24 hours.

Heat a heavy-based frying pan or a chargrill pan over medium heat, add the steak and fry for 2–3 minutes each side. Remove from the pan and allow to rest for a few minutes.

Wipe out the pan and return to the heat. Quickly add the tortillas to the dry pan and heat on both sides until warmed through. Divide among serving plates.

Thinly slice the steak and add to the tortillas, along with the avocado, onion and coriander. Top with chilli sauce and serve with lime wedges.

SERVES 4

Marinated skirt steak tacos

WHISKY-BRAISED BEEF SHORT RIBS

Short ribs have to be one of my favourite cuts of beef to cook with. They're super cheap, rich and fatty, and they come on the bone – a sure-fire combination for a flavour-packed dish. This recipe calls for a cup of whisky, which, along with the malt vinegar, adds a wonderful sharpness that cuts through the richness of the beef. That said, I wouldn't go adding a slug of your finest twenty-year-old single malt. A cheaper option works just fine – save the good stuff for sipping alongside your ribs!

2 kg beef short ribs (4–8 pieces)

salt and black pepper

115 g (½ cup) brown sugar

6 garlic cloves, finely chopped

250 ml (1 cup) whisky

125 ml (½ cup) malt vinegar

400 g can crushed tomatoes

Preheat the oven to 150°C.

Place the ribs, meat-side up, in a deep roasting tin and season generously with salt and pepper.

Put the sugar, garlic, whisky, vinegar and tomatoes in a large mixing bowl and whisk thoroughly to combine. Pour this mixture evenly over the ribs. Place a sheet of baking paper over the ribs, then cover the entire tin with foil. Pop the tin in the oven and roast for 2 hours.

Remove the foil and baking paper and baste the ribs with the sauce, then return the tin, uncovered, to the oven and roast for another 1–1½ hours, basting regularly. The meat is ready when it falls easily off the bone.

SERVES 4

COMM-UNITY

Join a community garden | Passata day
Cook a whole pig | Pickle party | Brew your own beer
Make a batch of real sausages
Build a wood-fired barbecue

Being a part of a community is a fundamental requirement for wellbeing. We humans are social creatures, and I don't mean the 'check out how many Instagram followers I have' type of social; I mean the 'face to face, sharing a meal and a conversation' type. Have you ever heard of the 'Blue Zone' diet? It refers to a collection of communities from around the world that have the longest natural life expectancy, thanks in part to their diet, although food isn't the only contributing factor. Each of these groups enjoys a rich community life, and the support and sense of belonging that comes with it. The good news is that you don't have to live on an island in the Mediterranean or off the coast of Japan to enjoy the benefits of a vibrant community life (though that would be nice), and to me, there's no finer vehicle for fostering community than food. Gardening is better with friends, preparing food is better with friends, and eating food is infinitely better with friends.

When it comes to growing your own food, the concept of 'self-sufficiency' gets thrown around a lot. The idea has always been appealing to me on paper – growing an abundance of vegetables, fruit and meat, and having a larder overflowing with the rewards of my own labour. But it wasn't until I was fumbling my way through learning how to manage a small farm that I realised the idea of self-sufficiency doesn't really go far enough. Although there were days when I would toil away without seeing another soul, most days would involve a visit to or from a neighbour. We'd share ideas, labour, food and a cup of something hot (or a bottle of something cold if the day was getting on). These were the people who shared my jubilation when a long-awaited harvest arrived, the people who helped me pickle, prep and pod, and the people I'd turn to when disaster struck. When I figured out that it was nigh on impossible and even somewhat foolish to try and grow everything myself, I focused on what I was good at and bartered with my neighbours for what they were good at.

Without these wonderful relationships my experience of growing food would have been quite solitary, completely lacking the life and vibrancy that made it so appealing. Food without people just isn't the same. To me, people (particularly your family and friends) are the backbone of the whole experience of food, from growing it and preparing it to the cherry on top: sitting down to share it. I came to realise that growing food isn't so much about self-sufficiency; it's more about community resilience and I reckon this idea applies whether you're a hobby farmer on 20 acres,

a commercial farmer on 2000 acres or a home farmer with a sunny little courtyard.

So if you've got a handle on growing and enjoy being in the kitchen, now's the time to bring these together with a bit of community. Having a local food community comes into its own when there is work to be done, whether it's dealing with a glut of produce or preparing a feast for family and friends. The time passes more quickly and the load seems lighter when you're working while chatting away with your mates.

If you already have a food community around you then keep doing what you're doing, but if you don't and you'd like to know where to start, you've come to the right place, my friend. I enjoy barbecues and dinner parties as much as anyone, but in my opinion the best days are those when there's a job to be done and you just so happen to be eating, drinking and being merry while you get on with it. This section of the book contains some of my favourite projects to bring a group of friends together and do something that's both fun and productive. Some of my fondest memories have been at get-togethers just like the ones described here. I certainly hope that they encourage and inspire you to make a few awesome memories with your nearest and dearest.

JOIN A COMMUNITY GARDEN

Not everyone has the luxury of being able to tend their own private garden, or maybe you like the idea of gardening but don't particularly want to nurture plants for months and months on end. Perhaps you do have a bit of space and a desire to garden but you don't have the foggiest idea where to begin and frankly find the whole thing a little overwhelming. If you fall into any of these categories, then allow me to introduce you to your new best friend: the community garden. These volunteer-run organisations tend a plot that is usually on public land, and open to members of the community to join in and either garden as an individual plot holder or as a part of the community garden collective.

There are numerous benefits to this type of gardening: you become an active member of a community, it encourages you to eat more vegetables, it lets you play a role in your own food security, you get to meet kindred gardening spirits from all walks of life, you can learn and share skills, and you can save buckets of money by pooling resources such as tools. I could go on, but I think you get the picture. There are hundreds of community gardens all over Australia, and if there isn't one near you, you could always get a band of like-minded souls together and start your own! If you're interested in joining a community garden, here are a few tips for how to go about it.

BE CLEAR ABOUT WHY YOU WANT TO JOIN A GARDEN

Is it for space to grow, acquisition of new knowledge, social connection, physical activity? Whatever your reasons, keep them in mind so that when you do find a garden you can be sure it satisfies your needs so you stay motivated.

TRACK DOWN SOME GARDENS IN YOUR LOCAL AREA

The Australian City Farms & Community Gardens Network (ACFCGN) (communitygarden.org.au) is a fantastic resource for all things community garden, including a guide to gardens in your area. Otherwise, try contacting your local council and local garden clubs.

GET IN TOUCH

Whether it be through social media, email or visiting the garden in person, it's essential to open the channels of communication. There's no need to commit to anything at this stage, but it's really helpful to have a chat to someone who's a regular at the garden; they can answer any questions you have and outline how you can get involved.

ATTEND AN OPEN GARDEN OR WORKING BEE

Most community gardens have a monthly working bee or open garden. This is usually the day where the garden is at its liveliest and is the perfect way to dip your toe in the water. You can meet the other gardeners, enjoy a cup of tea and a chat, and help out with any communal chores that need to be done around the place. If you're a little nervous, just remember that gardeners are probably the friendliest people around and are more than happy to show a newcomer the ropes.

JOIN UP

Once you've found a community garden that suits your needs and paid a visit to see how it all works, it's time to take the plunge and join up.

Every community garden is different and you may have access to your own plot straight away, you may have to go on a waiting list, or perhaps the whole garden is communal and there will be an expectation that you will contribute to its upkeep.

YOU ONLY GET OUT WHAT YOU PUT IN

This rings true for both gardens and community groups: they run on people's love, enthusiasm and effort. Look after your plot, help out on working bees, respect other people and their plots, and keep the tool shed tidy and you'll reap all the benefits that community gardens have to offer.

START YOUR OWN

If there's no community garden in your area, maybe it's time to take matters into your own hands! If you can muster up a couple of like-minded friends and put a proposal together, there's every chance you can start your own community garden. ACFCGN have detailed material on their website about how you can go about it.

AND
CLOSE GATE
WHEN LEAVING

PASSATA DAY

Enjoyed in the peak of summer, sun-ripened tomatoes are one of the great joys that repay vegetable gardeners for their sweat and toil. They are incredible eaten still warm from the sun, but they are also very easy to preserve, especially in the form of passata (which in less sexy speak simply means strained tomato puree). This basic sauce is a versatile pantry staple, maintaining the flavour of fresh tomatoes for year-round cooking, particularly hearty slow-cooked meals in the depths of winter. If you have any connection to Australia's Italian community, you've probably heard of or even attended a passata day; if you haven't, fear not – the process is very simple, and the volume of work is made all the easier by good company and a splash of wine.

Unless you're a gun tomato grower, you probably won't yield enough tomatoes to enjoy them fresh and make a year's worth of passata. Fortunately, towards the end of summer, tomatoes can be bought by the box at very reasonable prices as the commercial growers experience their glut. I'm not talking about the supermarket here; try to find a wholesaler that sells to the public, speak to your local greengrocer or have a chat with a tomato grower at a farmers' market and buy your tommies through them. Make sure the tomatoes you source are vine-ripened field tomatoes, preferably organic. Generally, roma or San Marzano are the best varieties for passata making.

To figure out how many tomatoes you'll need to make a year's supply of passata, think about how many 750 ml bottles of sauce you use in a week. My family of four uses about two bottles a week, which roughly translates to 100 bottles a year. It takes approximately 1 kg of tomatoes to fill a 750 ml bottle, so 100 kg (five 20 kg boxes) of tomatoes is more than enough to keep us well stocked. I know that seems like a lot, both to source and to process, but therein lies the beauty of communal preparation. You get to play detective as you hunt down the best tomatoes, then, when the big day arrives, you and your people get to spend quality time together, working and chatting, and then, hey presto! At the end of the day you have full bellies and hearts as well as a year's supply of tomato sauce. It's a tradition in the Italian community for good reason. Why not make it a tradition of your own?

WHAT YOU'LL NEED

Bottles and a capper/caps I find 750 ml beer bottles with crown seals are perfect for passata, although any sealable glass vessel will do the job. I like to use beer bottles because they are cheap and easy to find second hand, and using one type of vessel makes life a lot easier when you're dealing with such a large quantity of tomatoes. If you use beer bottles you'll also need a crown capper and caps. Cappers can be easily found second hand and caps can be purchased from home-brew suppliers. You'll also need to make sure all your bottles are spotlessly clean and sanitised ready for the big day.

Sanitiser To clean your bottles. They are easily available online or from home-brew suppliers. If you're only doing a smallish batch you can sterilise your bottles in the same way you would for making pickles and jams (boiling them, then putting them in a 110°C oven for 15 minutes, or running them through the dishwasher). But when you have a stack of bottles to get through, a liquid sanitiser like they use in home-brewing is the quickest method.

Large food-grade buckets or plastic containers Have a few of these around for sanitising bottles, washing tomatoes and managing the scraps and waste.

Tomatoes Field-grown vine-ripened saucing varieties like roma or San Marzano, preferably organic. Remember, to supply a family of four for a year you'll need about 100 kg.

A passata machine There are ways around buying and using a passata machine, but if you plan on processing a decent volume of tomatoes the initial investment will pay itself off very quickly. They tend to be a robustly made, one-off purchase; I'm hoping that my grandkids will have a turn at cranking ours.

Funnel Go for a stainless steel one with a wide mouth for transferring the passata to the bottles. This indispensable utensil will keep the bottles clean and get them filled quickly.

A huge stockpot or 44-gallon drum and a heat source The pot speaks for itself but the heat source needs to be strong enough to boil water for 40 minutes. This is to pasteurise the sauce once it's in the bottles.

Towels For lining the stockpot or drum to make sure the bottles don't knock together and smash during boiling.

Labels It may seem like overkill, but I like to label everything with the contents of the bottle and the date it was made. You'll be glad you did. I mean, it beats pouring beer into your bolognese or necking a bottle of tomato sauce after a hot day in the garden.

Wine Important for keeping the human machinery lubricated.

WHAT TO DO

In the days before Check that you have all your equipment and make sure it's clean and in working order. It also helps to prepare a space for the big day. You'll need enough room for all your workers, a few tables, the bottles, the tomatoes and your big pot. I find a single-car garage is ample.

On the day Invite everyone over first thing and have a quick cuppa, then get stuck in. You should aim to have all the bottles filled and being boiled before breaking for lunch – that way you can eat while the bottles pasteurise, and by the time you've finished and done the dishes, the bottles should be cool enough for everyone to label and take home.

1 Sanitise your clean bottles by making up a solution in a 20-litre bucket according to the instructions on your sanitiser. Soak the bottles for a couple of minutes, then place them upside-down on a rack to drip dry.

2 Wash the tomatoes.

3 Quarter the tomatoes and cut away rotten or discoloured bits.

4 Pass the tomatoes through your passata machine. The sauce will run out into your collecting bucket and the skins and seeds will push out the end of the auger. To get the most out of the tomatoes, I like to pass the skins and seeds through a second time for maximum juice extraction.

5 Using the funnel, transfer the juice to the bottles, leaving a 4 cm gap at the top.

6 Cap the bottles.

7 Place a towel on the base of your pot or drum to stop the bottles from rolling around and cracking. Gently place the bottles into the pot. You can arrange them standing up, or to fit more in, lay them down in a single layer, then add another towel, followed by another layer of bottles. Repeat until all your bottles are in or the pot is full. Fill the pot with water and bring it to a gentle boil, then let it bubble away for 40 minutes. Kill the heat and wait until the bottles are cool enough to be handled.

8 Remove the bottles from the water and wipe dry, then label and distribute them. Clean up and bask in the glory of your 12-month supply of delicious homemade passata.

COOK A
WHOLE PIG

So you're having a big shindig and your guest list is well and truly into the double digits – how on earth are you going to feed them all? When it comes to feeding a crowd, nothing beats cooking a whole animal. There's something deeply primal and satisfying (and perhaps a little disturbing to your vegetarian or vegan friends) about the sight and smell of meat cooking over coals. To the uninitiated, the process can seem a little intimidating, but it needn't be. With a few simple bits of kit, a lovely little free-range pig and some wood and charcoal, you'll have everything you need to feed up to twenty people. A quick trip to the hardware shop will sort out any materials you don't have.

WHAT YOU'LL NEED

Suckling pig To feed twenty or so people (with leftovers), you'll need a 12 kg free-range suckling pig, butterflied. Ask your butcher to do this for you.

Stanley knife For scoring the skin and fat. This lets the pig shrink a little as it cooks and helps with that all-important crackling.

Salt For rubbing into the skin.

Clean tea towels To cover the salted pig while it comes to room temp.

8 standard cement besser blocks These blocks are fire resistant and raise the reo mesh to a height where the pig can cook evenly.

Firewood To start your charcoal burning. Seasoned hardwoods like ironbark or red gum are my preference.

20 kg hardwood charcoal When cooking a pig I like to use charcoal rather than wood because it burns hot and slow and without much flame. I always go with pure hardwood charcoal as it doesn't have any additional binders or chemicals in it.

A shovel For moving your coals around.

A piece of reo mesh Reo mesh is the steel mesh that concreters use to add structural support to cement slabs. You can find it at hardware or building supply shops, but it comes in sheets much larger than you'll need here. Ideally, look for an off-cut at your local tip shop or try asking at a building site and just give it a good clean before you use it. You'll need a piece that's big enough to lay the pig on with a 30 cm border all round (about 1.5 metres × 1.5 metres).

Meat thermometer To make sure the meat is cooked through.

Thick gloves or tea towels To turn the pig over during cooking.

Foil To cover the pig while it rests.

TIPS

> Slow and steady wins the race, don't rush the cooking.

> To get a good indication if the heat is right, hold your hand above where the pig will cook. You should be able to keep it there for 5–10 seconds before it gets too hot.

> If you're feeling adventurous or are not a fan of pork, you could always try lamb, goat or chicken cooked in a similar way. Adjust the cooking times accordingly.

WHAT TO DO

1 A couple of hours before you plan to start cooking, remove the pig from the fridge and lay it flat on a clean work surface. Take your Stanley knife and score the skin of the pig, making sure you only cut down through the skin and fat, not the flesh. Rub a generous amount of salt into the scored skin, then cover with a couple of clean tea towels and let the pig come to room temperature.

2 Choose the spot where you'd like to cook your pig – it needs to be somewhere where the fire won't pose a risk. You can cook on the ground or on cement; just keep in mind that the spot will look a little worse for wear. Arrange four of the cement blocks standing upright in a rectangle. The other four blocks can be used to protect the fire from wind if it's a bit blowy. Place the reo mesh on the cement blocks.

3 Start fires with the firewood and a decent shovel-load of charcoal underneath where the shoulders and legs of the pig will sit. Once the charcoal is almost all white, spread it out a little using the shovel. Check that the coals are hot enough by holding your hands above them, just under the rio mesh – you should only be able to hold them there for a few seconds before it gets too hot.

4 Lay the pig, skin-side up, on the reo mesh, lining up the shoulders and legs with the two piles of charcoal.

5 While the pig is starting to cook, start another charcoal fire nearby so you always have a ready supply of hot coals to top up the cooking fire. Top up the coals under the pig every 30 minutes or so and keep cooking the pig, skin-side up, until the internal temperature of the thickest part of the leg reaches 60°C. This should take about 2 hours.

6 At this point, it's time to turn the pig over. With the help of a friend (and some thick gloves or a tea towel – the pig will be hot), lift it up and flip it over, then place it back on the reo mesh, skin-side down. Cook for another 30 minutes or so, until the internal temperature of the thickest part of the leg reaches 67°C.

7 Have a sneaky taste test with your mates!

8 Remove the pig from the fire, cover it with foil and let it rest away from the heat for 30 minutes. It will continue to cook after it comes off the heat, reaching the desired final temperature of about 70°C. Carve it up and serve it with some crusty bread rolls, sauerkraut and chilli sauce (see pages 148 and 162).

PICKLE PARTY

Sometimes when you're growing your own food you can find yourself suddenly going from having no produce at all to having so much that you don't know what to do with it! I'm sure anyone who has overzealously planted more than two zucchini plants can relate. Even if you don't grow your own food, when fruit and veggies are at the height of their season they are often sold so cheaply it makes you want to take advantage of it. This is why we preserve; we take something from a time of abundance and turn it into something tasty and shelf stable to enjoy when times are lean.

People have been preserving food in one form or another for more than 10,000 years. It's an easy process but the act of chopping up a glut of vegetables can be a little labour intensive. You know what I'm going to say. The best way to fill the pantry and use up surplus produce is to get a few friends together and have a pickle party. Sounds like a wild time, I know, but trust me: all you need to do is put on some tunes, get your chat happening and before you know it, that mountain of produce will be transformed into gleaming jars of flavour-packed goodness. The best thing is that when you're twisting the top off one of those jars months later, you'll be reminded of the good food, good folk and good times that made it all possible.

There are as many recipes for pickling as there are grains of sand on a beach, with every person, family and culture having a different take on what goes into the tastiest pickles. Luckily, if you're starting out, there is a basic ratio you can follow to get you on your way, which you can then customise to your liking. The quantities opposite will make enough liquid to fill six 500 ml jars but you can obviously increase the amount of liquid if you have more produce to pickle.

WHAT YOU'LL NEED

EQUIPMENT

Jars and lids 6 × 500 ml clean jars with lids

Baking trays For sterilising the jars

Fresh produce You'll need about 2 kg to go with this quantity of pickling liquid. See Tips for ideas.

Chopping boards and knives For preparing the veg.

Wide-mouthed funnel Go for a stainless steel one with a wide mouth for transferring the liquid to the jars.

A big, heavy-based saucepan or two For cooking the pickles if required and for boiling the sealed jars.

Tea towel To line your saucepan when boiling the jars of pickles — it will help prevent breakages.

Jar lifter or tongs A jar lifter can be purchased from kitchen supply stores. Alternatively you can use a pair of tongs and a steady hand.

INGREDIENTS

500 ml (2 cups) vinegar (white wine, distilled, apple cider or rice vinegar are my picks; steer clear of intensely flavoured vinegars like balsamic)

500 ml (2 cups) water (tap is fine)

2 tablespoons salt

2 tablespoons caster sugar

Your choice of flavourings (see Tips for ideas)

TIPS

Honestly, you can throw just about anything into a pickle jar! But if you're new to this, here are some suggested combos to get you started:

> Blanched green beans, coriander seeds and chilli

> Roasted beetroot, peeled and cut into wedges, caraway seeds and dill sprigs

> Carrots, cut into batons, cumin seeds and a few sprigs of oregano

> Zucchini, cut into long wedges, turmeric and fennel seeds

WHAT TO DO

1 First up, give all your jars and lids a wash in hot soapy water, then arrange them, mouth-side up, on a couple of clean baking trays. Preheat the oven to 120°C.

2 Prepare your fresh produce by cutting it into the desired shape and size, keeping in mind the dimensions of the jars you have sourced, as it will obviously need to fit in there!

3 Make your pickling solution by combining all the ingredients in a saucepan and bringing the liquid to the boil.

4 Sterilise your clean jars. Place the baking trays with the jars and lids in the preheated oven for about 20 minutes. Remove them from the oven and, once the jars are cool enough to handle, fill them with your chopped vegetables. This is a great step to get the kids involved with.

5 Use the funnel to pour in the pickling liquid, leaving a gap of about 5 mm at the top. Twist the lids on.

6 Line the bottom of your largest saucepan with the tea towel and place your jars of pickles in. Add enough water to the saucepan to completely submerge the jars. Place the saucepan over high heat, bring to the boil and leave it to bubble away for 10 minutes.

7 Use the tongs or jar lifter to carefully remove the jars from the pan and pop them on the bench to cool to room temperature.

8 Label your jars with the name of the pickles and the date they were made and distribute amongst your friends (keeping a few for yourself, of course). Store them in a cool, dark cupboard and use them within a year.

BREW YOUR
OWN BEER

In my experience, an air of both mystery and dread hangs over home-brewed beer. Mystery because it seems almost magical that you can take some grain, water, dried flowers and yeast and turn it into a magical brown elixir; this is compounded by the fact that when brewers speak of their craft, it's as though they are speaking another language. The sense of dread comes from the countless times a mate has brought their 'homebrew' to a party, and something akin to slightly fizzy swamp water hits your lips.

Brewing is an art that you can follow as far down the rabbit hole as you want in terms of expensive kits and elaborate recipes, so here's how to brew a beer using only whole ingredients, no extracts, and a minimum of equipment. The recipe on page 282 contains one type of malted grain and one type of hops – in brewing circles it's known as a SMaSH and it's a nice way to ease yourself into the world of all-grain brewing. You'll need a good chunk of a day for the brew, and a month's worth of patience for the fermentation before you can start necking your refreshing ales, but it will be worth the wait, I promise.

WHAT YOU'LL NEED

Some of the equipment and ingredients are quite specific but they're easy to find at home-brew shops or online.

EQUIPMENT

A huge saucepan or stockpot You'll need a 30-litre stainless steel pan with a lid.

Thermometer This is vital to make sure your water is at the right temperature to add the grains, and your beer is ready to pitch the yeast. A digital cooking thermometer will do the trick.

'Brew In A Bag' (BIAB) bag This is a fabric bag that sits in the pan and holds all the grains. It's an Australian innovation and makes small-batch home-brewing easier and more accessible. Buy readymade or, if you're handy on the sewing machine, you can make them out of the synthetic material voile (available in fabric stores).

A long spoon Stainless steel or wooden. Grab the longest one you've got.

An old blanket or sleeping bag This is to wrap around the saucepan while the malt grains are soaking to keep the water at a stable temperature.

A clean 20-litre bucket The BIAB bag goes in here after it comes out of the pan to catch any additional liquid that drains out.

A large esky or bucket with filled ice Large enough to sit the pot in.

Mesh strainer The larger, the better.

30-litre fermenter with bung and airlock The bung and airlock seals the bucket, while still allowing any gases produced during fermentation to safely escape the fermenter. It's way bigger than you need for this recipe but will be ready for you when you want to scale up your brews.

A small stainless steel funnel To help transfer the sugar into the bottles for secondary fermentation.

Bottles, bottle tops and a bottle capper You'll need 16 cleaned and sanitised long-neck bottles and 16 tops (see page 266 for instructions).

Bottling wand This is a simple and cheap valve mechanism to make filling your bottles a breeze.

INGREDIENTS

3 kg pale malt (2-row, ale), pre-milled

50 g Galaxy hops, divided into four batches of 12.5 g

2 teaspoons Safale US-05 dry yeast

80 g (⅓ cup) caster sugar

TIPS

> Scan second-hand websites or social media groups for people selling brewing gear to save money.

> Talk to your local home-brew supplies shop or join an online forum – experienced brewers are passionate and knowledgeable and usually very happy to help out a newbie.

> Make sure that your fermenter, bottling wand, bottles and caps are all spotlessly clean and have been sterilised before use. Use a brew gear sterilising solution, which can be picked up from a home-brew shop. Make up the solution as per the instructions and make sure all the surfaces that will come into contact with your beer get a good rinsing with the sterilising solution.

> Store the beer somewhere dark and cool and enjoy within 6 months.

WHAT TO DO

1 Fill your saucepan with 20 litres of water (measure it!), place it on the stove over high heat and heat it to 75°C.

2 Turn off the heat and carefully place the BIAB bag in the pan of hot water, making sure the mouth of the bag hangs over the rim of the pan. Add the grains and stir with the long spoon, making sure there are no clumps. Check the temperature – it needs to be as close as possible to 67°C. If it's a little hot, add a few ice cubes; if it's a little cool, place it back over the heat and gently bring it up to temperature.

3 Once the magic 67°C has been achieved, pop the lid on the pan and wrap the blanket around it (double check your stove is off!). Let it sit for an hour.

4 Remove the blanket and lid and lift out the brew bag, letting as much wort (liquid) come out of the grains as possible. Sit the bag in the bucket and set aside to drain further. Turn the heat back on under the pan and bring the wort to the boil, then add one batch of the hops. Continue boiling the wort for an hour adding the other batches of hops at the 40-, 50- and 60-minute marks. The excess liquid that drains out of bag into the bucket can be added at any time during the boil.

5 Put your esky or bucket filled with ice near the stove, then place the pan (lid on) in the esky. Pour water into the esky so that the pan is sitting in an ice bath. You want the temperature of the wort to come down to 20°C as quickly as possible.

6 Place the strainer over the mouth of your clean fermenter and gently pour the wort into it, making sure the last bit with all the debris doesn't go in. There should now be around 12 litres of wort in the fermenter. Add the yeast to the wort and use a clean spoon to give it a good stir, then seal up the fermenter. Place it somewhere dark that will stay between 15°C and 22°C and let it sit for 2 weeks.

7 When the 2 weeks is up, use the funnel to place 1 teaspoon of sugar in each of your long-neck bottles, then use the bottling wand to transfer the beer to the bottles. Fill them to the top – when the wand comes out you should have about a 2 cm gap at the top.

8 Use the bottle capper to seal the bottles, then place them somewhere dark between 15°C and 22°C for another 2 weeks to finish the carbonation process. Refrigerate and enjoy!

MAKE A BATCH OF
REAL SAUSAGES

Whatever happened to good sausages? Perhaps they went the way of many of the local butchers who made them and were supplanted by something cheaper and more convenient. Unfortunately, so much of what passes for a sausage today is merely a package for homogenised, fleshy oddities and what might be sawdust. The worst thing is these fauxsages have become so ubiquitous that we now willingly associate them with everything from a trip the hardware store to exercising our democratic rights.

A real sausage is a work of art – the perfect blend of meat and fat that explodes with flavour. If you don't live near a butcher that makes the real deal, then it's time to get a couple of friends together and make your own. The recipe below should give you about 150 sausages.

WHAT YOU'LL NEED

EQUIPMENT

Meat mincer Available from good kitchen supply stores, these can be temporarily mounted onto your kitchen bench. If you plan to do this regularly, it's worth investing in a decent-sized one (mine is by Italian company Tre Spade and it works a treat). I personally steer clear of mincers that mount to the front of stand mixers as they take a prohibitively long time to mince any sizeable volume of meat.

A couple of large stainless steel bowls and a baking tray For holding the minced meat after it comes out of the grinder.

Small frying pan For frying off a tester of the sausage mince.

A little olive oil For greasing the nozzle of the sausage stuffer and to fry up the sausage mince sampler.

Sausage stuffer This is a cylinder that pushes the meat through a nozzle into the sausage casing. You can get motorised models but I find the hand-cranked ones are more than ample for the home sausage maker. Available from good kitchen supply stores.

1 natural hog casing (about 20 metres long) Casings are available online or from your local butcher.

A clean needle This is to prick the raw sausages to allow any air to escape. I don't condone pricking sausages before cooking them (releasing all that precious fat into the pan) but in this case the holes re-seal as the sausages dry in the fridge.

INGREDIENTS

2 × 4.5 kg fatty free-range boneless pork shoulders

3 kg fatty free-range boneless pork belly

100 g (1 cup) fennel seeds

60 g (½ cup) dried chilli flakes

140 g (½ cup) salt

6 small bunches of sage, leaves picked and finely chopped

TIPS

> If you're not keen on buying your own mincer, head to your local butcher and have a chat with them. Let them know that you're making your own sausages and ask if they could mince up the shoulder and belly for you.

> Make sure you use free-range pork. Not only does it have more fat and better flavour, it means you won't be supporting an industry that raises animals in cramped, miserable conditions.

> Some other flavour combinations that you could try are:

> Red wine and black pepper
> Port and chilli
> Thyme and garlic
> Chilli and cheese

WHAT TO DO

1 Before you start, make sure that all your equipment and ingredients are as cold as you can get them without freezing the meat. A couple of hours before you begin, chuck the mincer, a couple of stainless steel bowls and the meat in the freezer. When the meat is firm and cold, but not frozen, cut it up into rough 3 cm cubes and put it in one of the stainless steel bowls. Return to the freezer for 30 minutes.

2 Set up the mincer with a coarse plate and mince the cold meat into the second stainless steel bowl or a baking tray.

3 Add the fennel seeds, chilli, salt and sage and give everything a good mix with your hands. Pop a small frying pan on the stove over medium–high heat and add a little olive oil. Roll a bit of the mixture into a ball and cook it up to test the seasoning. It's better to know for sure that your sausages are going to be delicious before you stuff the meat into casings. Adjust the seasoning if necessary, then return the meat to the freezer while you clean up your work area.

4 Set up the sausage stuffer and load the mince into the cylinder. Turn the crank until the mince reaches the end of the nozzle.

5 Rub a little olive oil on the nozzle, then gently work the casing onto the nozzle. Once all the casing is on, tie a small knot in the end so that it sits flush with the end of the nozzle.

6 Keep a light but firm grip on the casing, and steadily turn the crank. The mince should fill the casing and not leave any air gaps, but be careful not to fill it too tightly otherwise the casing will split. Fill the entire length of the casing, leaving a bit of a tail, then tie another knot where the meat ends.

7 Decide what length you'd like your finished sausages to be by pinching the unportioned sausage with one hand and twisting with the other. Repeat until all of your sausages are portioned.

8 Place the sausages on a clean tray and prick them all over with a clean needle. Place the tray in the fridge and chill the uncovered sausages for couple of hours, then transfer them to a container. You can store the sausages in the fridge for up to a week or freeze them for a couple of months.

BUILD A WOOD-FIRED BARBECUE

Having a barbecue is almost a prerequisite to the Australian lifestyle. Hot summers, cold beers and long evenings lend themselves to cooking outdoors. But something has been lost along the way – a flavour, an aroma that you simply can't achieve by twisting a gas knob. We're missing the magic of a wood fire.

Now I'm not going to stand here and argue that a wood-fired barbecue is just as convenient as a gas barbecue, because it's not, but the whole process – the crackling fire and the flavour of food cooked over embers of burning wood – is infinitely more rewarding. If you've got a bit of space in your backyard, then you can build a super-simple wood barbecue out of cement blocks and a metal grate for just over $150 if you're buying all the materials brand new (easily done from a building supplies or hardware store). This is as simple as it gets and, as a bonus, it can be packed up and moved around if you like!

WHAT YOU'LL NEED

A shovel A solid long-handled shovel for getting rid of the grass under your barbecue site and for shifting coals around.

23 standard cement besser blocks Look for blocks that are 390 mm × 190 mm.

2 half cement besser blocks These need to be 190 mm × 190 mm.

1 metal grate About 1 metre × 1 metre.

8 cement besser block caps These caps cover the holes of the cement block so that you can rest your tongs and things on them without worrying about them falling in! They need to be 390 mm × 190 mm.

WHAT TO DO

1 Find a nice levelish patch of ground (about 1.2 square metres) and use the shovel to remove the grass. You don't have to dig very far down, just enough to get to bare earth. You want your barbecue to be as level as possible and, as this will be the foundation, you want to spend the time getting your bare-earthed square just right.

TIPS

> For best results, use seasoned hardwood, such as ironbark or red gum, for your fire.

> Keep a fire burning to one side of the barbecue and use a shovel to move coals to the other side.

> Avoid cooking directly over the flame as this will be too hot, causing your food to burn rather than cook through. For best results, wait until the fire has burned down to coals.

> You can cook so much more than snags and steaks on your barbecue. Try my barbecued butterflied chicken on page 216, but also just about any of your favourite veg. Even watermelon (see page 204)!

2 Stand where you'd like the front of your barbecue to be and lay three cement blocks along the left edge of your foundation and three blocks along the right side. These will be the sides of your barbie.

3 Join the two rows by placing two cement blocks along the back edge, forming the back of the barbie. Give all the blocks a little shuffle if required so they are all touching nice and flush.

4 Begin the second layer of blocks by placing three blocks along the back row, then two blocks each along the left and right sides. Then place the two half blocks at the front of the left and right sides.

5 Place the metal grate on the blocks, making sure the back edge of the grate sits flush with the back edge of the cement blocks. Put the final layer of blocks on top, using the same pattern as the first layer: three blocks along each side and two at the back.

6 Place the cement besser block caps on top of the cement blocks.

7 Build a fire under the grate, then let it burn down to coals.

8 Get cooking!

THANK YOU

First of all, I have to thank my gorgeous wife, Alicia, for your patience, perseverance and unwavering support, all of which made writing this book possible. Thank you from the bottom of my heart. I love you.

I'd also like to express my deepest gratitude to the good folk at Plum and the production team that brought this unruly gaggle of ideas and recipes to fruition. Thank you all for your support, encouragement and outstanding expertise. Together we have created such a beautiful book. I'm deeply proud of it and I hope you are too.

Thank you Mary for taking a punt on this book and for not berating me when we bumped into each other at day-care pickup and I was behind deadline.

Thank you Jane for your patience, gentle nudging and for expertly steering this project from the seed of an idea to a wholly tangible thing of beauty.

Thank you Rachel for your eternal patience while waiting for me to answer your editorial queries, and for distilling my rants into their final intelligible form.

Thank you Chris for perfectly capturing the magic as it happened and for bringing the recipes to life in such vibrant imagery.

Thank you Lee for making everything look so much more beautiful than I ever could, and for teaching me the coins under the plate trick.

Thank you Trisha for creating the gorgeous aesthetic of this book and for making it such a beautiful object.

Thank you Emma for your humour and hard work during the food shoot, even while heavily pregnant. Seems I can't write a book without you!

Finally, I need to thank you, the reader. Thanks for picking up this book and reading it. The world needs more people to grow and cook their own food.

GLOBAL CONVERSION CHART

Measuring cups and spoons may vary slightly from one country to another, but the difference is generally not enough to affect a recipe. All cup and spoon measures are level.

One Australian metric measuring cup holds 250 ml (8 fl oz), one Australian tablespoon holds 20 ml (4 teaspoons) and one Australian metric teaspoon holds 5 ml. North America, New Zealand and the UK use a 15 ml (3-teaspoon) tablespoon.

LIQUID MEASURES

One American pint = 500 ml (16 fl oz)
One Imperial pint = 600 ml (20 fl oz)

CUP	METRIC	IMPERIAL
⅛ cup	30 ml	1 fl oz
¼ cup	60 ml	2 fl oz
⅓ cup	80 ml	2½ fl oz
½ cup	125 ml	4 fl oz
⅔ cup	160 ml	5 fl oz
¾ cup	180 ml	6 fl oz
1 cup	250 ml	8 fl oz
2 cups	500 ml	16 fl oz
2¼ cups	560 ml	20 fl oz
4 cups	1 litre	32 fl oz

DRY MEASURES

The most accurate way to measure dry ingredients is to weigh them. However, if using a cup, add the ingredient loosely to the cup and level with a knife; don't compact the ingredient unless the recipe requests 'firmly packed'.

METRIC	IMPERIAL
15 g	½ oz
30 g	1 oz
60 g	2 oz
125 g	4 oz (¼ lb)
185 g	6 oz
250 g	8 oz (½ lb)
375 g	12 oz (¾ lb)
500 g	16 oz (1 lb)
1 kg	32 oz (2 lb)

LENGTH

METRIC	IMPERIAL
3 mm	⅛ inch
6 mm	¼ inch
1 cm	½ inch
2.5 cm	1 inch
5 cm	2 inches
18 cm	7 inches
20 cm	8 inches
23 cm	9 inches
25 cm	10 inches
30 cm	12 inches

OVEN TEMPERATURES

CELSIUS	FAHRENHEIT
100°C	200°F
120°C	250°F
150°C	300°F
160°C	325°F
180°C	350°F
200°C	400°F
220°C	425°F

CELSIUS	GAS MARK
110°C	¼
130°C	½
140°C	1
150°C	2
170°C	3
180°C	4
190°C	5
200°C	6
220°C	7
230°C	8
240°C	9
250°C	10

INDEX

A Plum book

First published in 2019 by
Pan Macmillan Australia Pty Limited
Level 25, 1 Market Street,
Sydney, NSW 2000, Australia

Level 3, 112 Wellington Parade,
East Melbourne, Victoria 3002, Australia

Design by Trisha Garner
Illustrations by Mila Balzhieva
Typesetting by Kirby Jones
Editing by Rachel Carter
Index by Helena Holmgren
Photography by Chris Middleton
Prop and food styling by Lee Blaylock
Food preparation by Paul West and Emma Roocke
Colour reproduction by Splitting Image Colour Studio
Printed and bound in China by 1010 Printing International Limited

A CIP catalogue record for this book is available from the National
Library of Australia.